DESIGNS IN THIS BOOK
HAVE BEEN SEEN ON:

HGTV TINY HOUSE BIG LIVING | SEASON 1 EPISODE 14

ARCHITIZER A+ AWARD WINNER 2016

DWELL ONLINE 2016

COSMOPOLITAN ONLINE 2016

MODERN IN DENVER MARCH 2013

ARCHDAILY MULTIPLE OCCASIONS

LUXURY HOME QUARTERLY FALL 2011

B1 MAGIZINE FALL 2013

PRAISE FOR THE CREATIVITY CODE:

"Whether I'm talking to Fortune 500 CEOs or Silicon Valley startup founders, they are all saying that innovation and creativity are the things they want most from their workforce. In this day and age creativity is the must-have skill that will propel anyone's career regardless of their profession. "The Creativity Code," teaches you specific concepts that drive creativity, uses real world examples, and provides a hands on guide to make sure you can apply it."

KEVIN KRUSE, NEW YORK TIMES BESTSELLING AUTHOR

"The creative process can be challenging to teach, systematize, and study. For many of us the process of developing a concept, making it tangible, and narrating its story is extremely personal. In the "Creativity Code", Alex Gore delicately introduce the complexities of the design process in a straight-forward, coherent, manner. A thought provoking read for the most veteran creatives to the beginners."

JEFFREY A. PINHEIRO, AIA : ARCHITECT
STUDIO.BAD ARCHITECTS

"From proportion and scale to sustainable chicken coop and a "skyscraper that grows", Alex Gore and Lance Cayko take you on a wild journey through antiquity to the modern day in search of the key to creativity. Anyone wanting to unleash their maximum creativity would do well to study The Creativity Code. "

ENOCH SEARS, AIA : ARCHITECT
BUSINESS OF ARCHITECTURE

ABOUT THE AUTHOR:

Alex Gore is the co-founder of the Architecture firm F9 Productions Inc. with Lance Cayko.

At North Dakota State University, he earned a Masters of Architecture, and a Masters in Construction Management degree while enlisted in the Army National Guard. While in Architecture school he won many competitions, and was awarded the Alpha Rho Chi Medal, bestowed by the faculty to the one student at each architecture Univeristy who best exemplifies leadership, service, and the promise of professional merit.

After college he was employed at the world famous architecture firm Studio Daniel Libeskind, before cofounding the firm F9 Productions. The firm is a leading BIM (Building Information Modeling) provider, and is currently designing hundreds of homes.

Lance and Alex teach at the University of Colorado, Boulder in the Architectural Engineering Department, and the Environmental Design Department. Their work has been featured on HGTV and can be seen in Magazine stands around the world. Recently they have been awarded the Architizer A+ Award.

THE CREATIVITY CODE

YOUR GUIDE TO:
ARCHITECTURE, DESIGN & DISCOVERING YOUR INNER DAVINCI

BY:

ALEX GORE

WITH LANCE CAYKO

978-0-9979275-1-1: HARDCOVER
978-0-9979275-2-8: PAPERBACK
978-0-9979275-3-5: EBOOK

EDITOR: Ann Maynard, Command+Z Content
COVER AND INTERIOR DESIGN: Alexander Gore

Creativity, Design, Architecture

Thanks to:

My parents, Keith and Sheri, the foundation of my life
My siblings, Wendy, Zach, and Corey
Grandma Graves, a shining star
Lance, this is your work as much as it is mine
The wonderful teachers at NDSU, and Century High School
The students at CU, Boulder who are an inspiration
And,
Anni, my always supportive and encouraging wife.

Readers Guide

This book builds sequentially up from a solid foundation. It is broken into three themed parts: Learn, Design, Live, with each part having three chapters.

In **Part One** | Learn, you will discover the design principles and process that can unleash your inner Da Vinci. Here you will learn how to solve problems by finding the root causes, and understand the value of shaping the process.

Part Two | Design. provides examples to enhance your understanding of the principles and processes in the previous chapters. Ranging from small to large these examples prove that the creative process is capable of creating real world change, and shows the future path of architecture.

Part Three | Live, provides guides, checklist, and reveals the secret of design, and peels the lessons out of this book to applies them to your life through encouraging action!

The **Appendix** is not to be taken lightly; it is a course in design and sketching. It is the first step in truly transforming your ideas to reality.

While it is recommended to read this book in order, I understand the desire to bounce around and encourage a little creativity:). My favorite chapter is "What if a building could grow?" No. 6 (so either skip ahead or don't quit until you get there). Mixing design chapters between principles and process chapters can be a good way to get the creative juices flowing. While the book is written to be read in order, it only requires a little extra

100%
FREE

CREATIVITY **VIDEO** COMPANION COURSE:

In order for this book to have an impact on your learning, I have included guides and checklist to apply to the projects you take on. To aid in this endeavor, I have also created an online portal so that you can print and save these items to use at your convenience. Follow the link to get the free resources.

There you will find: Website, Photoshop, Sketchup tutorials, and more to help put creativity into practice. Learning these tools gives you access to the creative economy. All of them are free of charge except for the specialized architectural Revit course.

www.alexandergore.com/bookresources

TABLE OF CONTENTS

What is Creativity?

Do you have to be born with it?
Can it be nurtured?
Are only artist creative?
Find out why creativitiy is in all of us.

Introduction | **WHAT IS CREATIVITY?**

The longer I live the more beautiful life becomes. If you foolishly ignore beauty, you will soon find yourself without it. Your life will be impoverished. But if you invest in beauty, it will remain with you all the days of your life.

Frank Lloyd Wright

In the summer of 2013, my business partner Lance and I met with the Environmental Design Director at the University of Colorado, Boulder. Our business was growing, and we were looking for employees. After some discussion about what our firm does and how we conduct business, the director threw us a curveball: "Can you teach the engineers how to design?"

She explained that they needed an instructor for an engineering course taught within the department. "A handful of people have taught the course in the past without much success. We're struggling to find a method that works."

The goal was to teach freshmen engineering students how to sketch, hand draft, and design. We also needed to teach them to use Revit, a computer-aided design program, and equip them with the technical skills they'd need in the professional world. The department needed an instructor who could teach all the requirements. More than that, they needed someone who could teach engineers to tap into their creativity. It was a tall order, and we accepted the role on the spot.

Our process was simple. We borrowed from my military background and applied the "crawl, walk, run" method of training. We first showed the students sketching, design, and computer skills in lecture; this was the crawl phase. Then in the lab, they tackled the same problems themselves. For example, drawing a room, sketching out a design, or modeling a cabin in the computer program we used. That step completed the walk phase.

The final step after they had mastered the skills, was to run. We then gave them their own project, letting them pick what they wanted to design. The students were more engaged and passionate in the work because they had the freedom to create what they wanted. But passion isn't enough; they also needed good tools. We gave the class access to all the tools, templates, and materials we use at our professional firm. Access to ample resources allowed them to leapfrog over most of the hurdles in other classes.

The "crawl, walk, run" method of creativity equipped our students with a foundation of understanding from which they could build what they wished—and it is the same approach I'll be teaching in this book. Even if the least you get out of this book is a new lens for you to see and analyze the world, I will be happy. But we are aiming higher than that. **This book seeks to show you how to shape opportunities out of obstacles, create patterns out of chaos, and show you how to turn intangible ideas into concrete reality.**

Since we have been teaching, the class has been a roaring success. Students often praise it as their favorite course. One student said the class kept her from dropping out of college. Each semester the buzz and excitement during the first day grows. At the end of each semester, we ask guests to sit in on the final presentation and have them critique the students' work. A professor from the Environmental Design Department once stood up at the end of the class and told the students he wished they could be in his third-year architecture studio.

This book initially started out as most architecture books do. It opened with my bio and then explained a particular project in my portfolio. But that wasn't the book I wanted to write. That book could not provide you with the transformational impact that we achieved in the class.

The book will explain, explore, and teach the process behind the designs. It will communicate the power of creativity, and show you how to use it in your own life. It's going to show you how to bring your intangible ideas into the real world.

This book is about how to shape the system within which you operate. It addresses the designer as well as the outcome. I believe this book will not just be useful for those who design, but for those who want to understand themselves.

WHAT IS CREATIVITY?

"Creatives could make unexpected connections
and see patterns in daily life,
even those lacking high intelligence or good grades."

99% Invisible podcast "The Mind of an Architect"

Creativity is the ability to make new things or think of new ideas. (1) It is part art, part rip off, part imagination, and part soul. It is the idea that stands alone, the shadow behind the thought, the spark that creates the idea.

Tina Seelig is an author and Stanford professor. She explains that creativity is a tool for solving problems with infinite answers (2). She points out that in grade school teachers ask students to solve problems like 5+5=? These problems have one correct answer. The questions get more complicated over time, but there is always only one right answer.

Creative people look at the world through a different lens. They look at problems from different angles. For example, instead of asking, what is five plus five? They ask, what two numbers add up to 10?

$$? + ? = 10$$

Here you can see there are infinite answers. 5+5, 3+7, 2+8, 5.5+4.5, 7.3+2.7, 6.24+3.76, -4+15, etc. Creativity leans more on investigating the questions you ask first, before seeking a solution.

Rational thinking is convergent thinking, whereas creative thinking is divergent. Most people think creativity comes from a guru, a spiritual journey, psychedelic drugs or that you need to be an "artist" of some type. Many believe if you are not in painting or music creativity isn't worth the cost of acquiring.

I am not of this persuasion. Like Robert Green, I believe creativity is in the mud, the dirt, and the grime of daily life. It is not outside of you, but through your work that you will find the structure on which to hang your creativity hat. Your creativity connects to who you are. (3)

And you can be both! Elon Musk, a hyper-rational thinker, has created three of the most creative companies of our era: PayPal, SpaceX, and Tesla. He is the perfect illustration of what is possible when the engineer and the artist are one. Our world needs more of this kind of thinking as we continue to progress.

The power of design and creativity is here to stay. Apple, AirBnB, Twitter, and a plethora of new businesses have shown how great design can outperform more established, deeper-pocketed firms. In today's era, you not only must be able to come up with an excellent idea and be able to convey and convince others of its merit, but often you must even produce it yourself. **Now more than ever, design matters.**

As for me, my work is in the field of Architecture. I earned a Masters Degree in Architecture and then a second Master's Degree in Construction Management. I used to work for a world-renowned architect Daniel Libeskind and co-founded an Architecture firm, F9 Productions with my business partner Lance Cayko. He and I developed most of the examples and thoughts in this book together. Over the years we have forgotten who has come up with what, so you can attribute the thoughts and ideas in this book to both of us.

To me, architecture is more than a roof over my head and fancy buildings in magazines. It is a reflection of society. Art made of stone, steel, and glass. It is the culmination of the masses. Every great piece of architecture had both a great architect and a great client. In my experience, the client and team we are working with are just as important in making the design amazing as I am.

> "The mother art is architecture. Without an architecture of our own we have no soul of our own civilization."
>
> **Frank Lloyd Wright**

In this book, architecture serves as a physical example of the creative process. Creativity can be abstract and sometimes hard to grasp, but buildings are physical manifestations of ideas and the process that formed them. The design process is how creative ideas become concrete realities.

What we do and what we produce—be it architecture or accounting, manual labor or service—our results are a mirror into our internal process. This book is about creativity, design, and architecture, but it is also about you the reader and how you can transform an idea into something tangible. It is about how to create your reality through the tools of the design trade. It is a lens through which to view life—one of many, but important nonetheless.

In this book, I hope you see examples that will inspire you, and ideas that will excite you. Good design is visual storytelling. It clarifies ideas, and can cement your voice in the world. For 15 years I have been creating designs for my clients and myself. I've been winning competitions, getting published, and working for top firms in the world. Now I want to help you create make your ideas become reality.

PART 1
LEARN

"Tell me and I forget, teach me and I may remember, involve me and I learn."

Benjamin Franklin

Creative
Principles

If you know how to shape the system you operate in, you will know how to get the resutls you want. Rules and systems can be freeing if used correctly. If you understand the priciples behind the rules you will know why, when, and if to break them.

Ch. 1 | **THE CREATIVE PRINCIPLES**

You have to learn the rules of the game. And then you have to play better than anyone else.

Albert Einstein

Creativity pulls strongly from the visual part of the brain. Despite that fact, the time and training necessary to develop these skills are often overlooked. Fortunately, visual thinkers comprise over half of the population. You, like many others, might have a visual acuity yet to be released. In this chapter and the next, I'll present you a sort of "Design Toolbox" that you can use to develop your skills.

Many non-fiction books offer systems for success. These prescriptions boil down to a list of steps (often in an easy to remember mnemonic device) that aims to solve a particular problem. The challenge with design, however, is that normally the problem is not clearly defined. A one-size-fits-most system isn't what you need.

So, this chapter is going to be a little different. I'm going to introduce different approaches that you can use to solve a specific problem. This chapter will illustrate the concepts of creativity using architectural examples to engage the visual portion of your mind. If you are not in the architectural field, be sure to pause after each section and reflect how the idea might interact in your area of study.

The design process has two main avenues, which mirror our mind: rationalization and creativity. Each of us tends to put emphasis on one side more than the other. Clarity comes from understanding both sides of your brain, and combining them to create something from your imagination. This chapter explores the creativity tools you can use to both build and assess your designs. These are Flow, Connection, and Contrast.

FLOW

Flow appeals to us on an intuitive level because it mimics nature. The problem is that it is hard to define, hard to teach, and you only know it when you see it—and that makes flow one of the most challenging ideas to master.

Novices see experts use this technique and attempt it themselves without realizing the effort it takes to make flow work. Flow often takes iteration after iteration after iteration after ITERATION to get it right.

Frank Gehry is one of the best architects at demonstrating this type of design. On the next page is an image of the Marques de Riscal hotel. What some people might not know is that it might take hundreds of attempts and many models to achieve this form. It takes time, dedication, effort, resolve, talent and taste to make flow work.

The process of iteration allows an idea to incubate in your mind. This incubation period allows the idea to penetrate your subconscious, where it forms new connections and creates stronger bonds between ideas.

To find useful ideas, it can be a good strategy to explore without aim, just seeking whatever captures your interest. This 'letting go' can be scary, making exploration a practice that only the practiced tend to follow.

David Straker (5)

Marques de Riscal hotel
Photo by: igorre1696: https://www.flickr.com/photos/igorre1969/2865176214/

Allow yourself to explore. Go with the flow. Let your mind wander without fear or hesitation. Sketch it out, and then do it again. Frank Gehry is always trying to come up with shapes and forms people have never seen before. He doesn't just accept the first thing or idea that comes to mind. Instead, Gehry tests the shape and form of his design. He'll even crumple up pieces of paper or toss paper airplanes at his models to see what works.

Flow comes through skill, and skill requires practice. The easiest way to begin designing with flow is through sketching. If you are hesitant about your sketching skills, see the appendix for some lessons to get you started in sketching.

Computer aided design software can also help you bring a flow idea into reality. The software you use will depend on your profession. Links to

Photoshop and Revit lessons are included in Chapter Nine.

CONNECTION

The success or failure of a building, an idea, or a product lies in its ability to connect with you. Connection happens when a designed object embodies an idea in tangible form. It's the relationship between inanimate object to an abstract idea such as love, beauty, history, power, trust, technology, etc.

Historically, religions have used symbolism to connect to their congregation. Christian church plans often take the shape of the cross. The design unites parishioners to the central theme of the religion: Jesus's sacrifice.

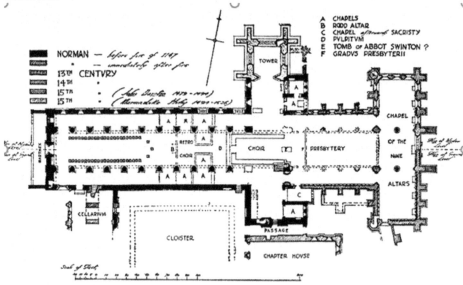

Gothic Church Plan. **Photo by** Dr. Alison Stones: http://www.medart.pitt.edu/image/England/fountains/Plans/Fountains-plans.html

Daniel Libeskind's Holocaust Museum in Berlin is a reflection of the harsh and chaotic reality of the plight of Jews during World War II. In contrast to the "angels in the architecture" Paul Simon sang about, Libeskind's museum has beautifully woven despair in the design. Metal faces line the floor as an exhibition of the potent reality of this oppressive time in history. Design can also convey a message. In designing federal

The Berlin Jewish Museum
Photo by Tom De Freston: http://www.tomdefreston.co.uk/artist/5057/berlin-the-jewish-museum/1dsfghjfd

buildings, there is often a mandate to convey justice, safety, and a sense of protection. The look of the building must conveys trust between a nation and its citizens. Conventionally classical architecture was used to communicate the genesis of democracy and it roots in justice. Over time this mandate has manifested in different forms. On the net page you can see the evolution of designs. While each building looks different and has distinct style, they each convey power. The lower right building by Morphosis Architecture has a sort of Death Star feel, but still speaks to the strength of the government.

People often like to connect to something larger than themselves. To do this, you could try to make your design convey awe or even inspire.

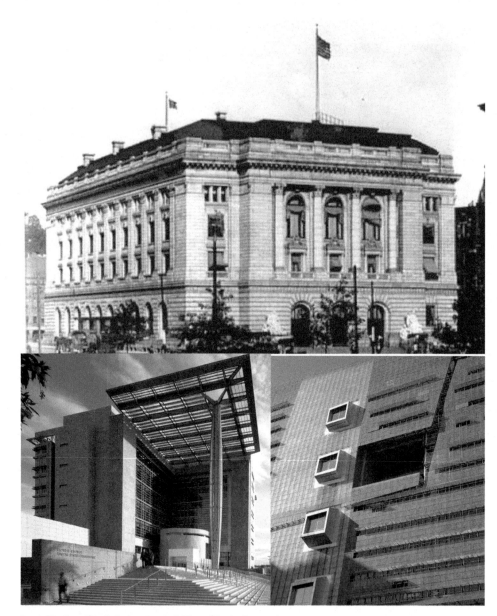

Top: Federal Building - Post Office **Photo by** Unknown
http://www.provlib.org/providence-buildings/federal-building-post-office
Bottom Left: Cannon Design - Lloyd D. George U.S. Courthouse and Federal
Building, Las Vegas, NV. **Photo by** Esto Photographics: http://cannon.7pwiu5hqygi
gvu1w3lmtyxkscr5rqnxrk5c1hjll7ke.netdna-cdn.com/assets/CAN0024_N22_web.jpg
Bottom Right: U.S. Federal Building in San Francisco **Photo by:** Tom Morris: https://
commons.wikimedia.org/wiki/File:San_Francisco_Federal_Building_side_detail.jpg

While these concepts are close, they have slight differences. Awe comes from a place of mystery. People want to know how it works. The CCTV Tower by Rem Koolhaas in China folds in on itself, creating a sort of chair-like cantilever that keeps one wondering how such a shape is possible.

Left: CCTV Tower. Photo by Killan Evang
Right: Chrysler Building Photo by Highsmith, Carol M.,

Inspiration fills people with pride. It motivates them to do or be something more than they thought they could. Take for example, the Chrysler Building in New York. It is a beautiful combination of scale and sophistication. More than that it's an iconic landmark and unmistakable representative of one of the most influential cities in the U.S. It does this through its height and icon tower, whos shape was inspired by the tip of a pensil and the rims of a tire.

The connection you create in your design is your choice. It could be the city's heritage, a company's brand, or an abstract concept. Whatever you choose, try to unify and connect your design with the thought or emotion behind it. Explore different options and themes. But know that whether you are writing a story, sketching a building, or marketing a product, you need to connect the external (form, function) to the internal (emotion). In other words, needing a home is different than needing to feel comfortable in that new home. Design bridges this gap.

EXAMPLE:

Years ago we used to design business cards. One of my favorites was one we made for a lighting designer.

Normally business cards are white, one-sided, with the company name, position, and contact info. They make little attempt to foster connection through the look and feel of the card. But can business cards connect with us? Can they create an emotional response? Can the exchange of cards create a moment between people? Yes, yes, and yes.

The card pictured below is a great example of how good design helps us convey an idea. The front features only the client's name colored

Image by: F9 Productions.

APPLICATION: Think of an idea you are trying to convey. How can you use design and visual thinking to communicate that idea?

with the the full spectrum of light, with the center "L" highlighted like a lightbulb, all set on a black background. The concept of color and light comes through in this card design, connecting lighting design with the client.

CONTRAST

Contrasting is a great tool that can add value to your design when used well. Its primary function is to highlight/emphasize a major difference. What you choose to contrast often becomes the focus.

In the previous example the colored text was contrasted by the black background. This distinction reinforced the idea of "light." Contrast can also convey depth. When sketching objects that are closer you can use heavier lines and darker shading to contrast from objects that are farther away. When entering a building, you can lower the ceiling of the entrance thus providing a feeling of compression and transition. You can release that tension by immediately opening up to a taller space after the entry.

Contrast works best when you set up a pattern that you can break. For example, a lone tower becomes more recognizable and compelling when sitting in the presence of shorter buildings.

It is best to use contrast to highlight an important aspect of the design. In buildings, this could be a stairwell, a large space, or a meaningful change.

For example, in the house on the next page, the main floor level consists of the kitchen, dining, and living room. The upper floor master bedroom opens to below. To highlight the change in function, I decided to use wood in contrast against the modern concrete of the rest of the house, which gave a "tree-fort"-like feel to the room. To me, it is a child's dream come true.

On a grander scale, a museum's design could be set to contrast the architecture surrounding it. Consider the way the Guggenheim Museum in

Image by: F9 Productions.

SPACE	VALUE CHANGE
1) The Entrance.	Compression: Large space outside, low ceiling inside.
2) The Kitchen.	Security and warmth: People often gather in the kitchen to relax. Warmth comes from the choice of materials: wood, columns, beams and ceilings.
3) The Living Room	Openness: Compression from the kitchen and entrance gets released in the living room via tall ceilings and large windows. Completing the value change loop.

Bilbao, Spain, and the Beijing National Stadium (also known as "The Bird's Nest") contrast themselves from the community.

Another important concept to remember in Contrast is the idea of value change. If we were to think about it in theater terms, your building is one scene inside the "play" of the city. The transitions between spaces and rooms would be the "beats." (6)

Contrast and value change brings interest, energy, and life to designs. When designing, ask each space, PowerPoint slide, section on a poster (top, middle, and bottom) what value they want to convey and how it relates to the whole.

SUMMARY:

Creativity is successful when it combines unique ideas to everyday problems. The first step in this process is to have a thorough understanding of what you are trying to solve. (More on that in the Design Process Chapter.) Then let your experience and the environment guide you to the solution. You can increase this capability by using the following tools to connect and engage your subconscious.

1) **FLOW**: Use iteration to uncover a hidden solution.

    A. Find your inspiration: nature, history, ideas, etc.

    B. Develop your skills: sketching, painting, and computer programs.

2) **CONNECTION**: Connect the essence of an idea with the elements in your design using. For example here are some ideas you can use to connect emotionally to your design.

    A. Symbolism

    B. Awe/Inspiration

  C. Justice/Safety

  D. Light

  E. Etc.

The key here is to determine what you want your design to say. It could embody the history or tradition of a place. Your design could convey strength or sleekness; it could be inviting like a resort, or intimidating like a prison. Don't limit yourself. Designs can imitate life with all of its emotions, hopes, dreams, and fears. Ask yourself what does strength look like, how does sleekness feel?

3) CONTRAST: Use scale, color, texture, shape, and positioning to distinguish key elements.

  A. Highlight

  B. Emphasis

  C. Value change and beats

To remember these principles, you can put the words in a phrase. "Creativity is about **Finding Connection through Contrast.**"

Creativity reveals ideas through unique ways. How can you relate a concept, emotion, or meaning in a building, a poster, product, song, or a story? Flow, Connection, and Contrast are the tools you can use to create a more beautiful world.

Rational Principles

Can creativity come from rationality?
Can we connect the left and right brain for better results? I believe so, on the preceding pages are tools and examples on how to rationally be creative. Remember these design examples are a new language you can apply to your feild.

Ch. 2 | **RATIONAL PRINCIPLES**

Often creativity is thought to come at the expense of rationality. These two concepts seem exclusive or even counterproductive to each other. To be creative you must free yourself from shackles of rationality. Likewise, the rational problem-solving process should cast aside creative endeavors that are a waste of time. Not only is this notion false, but it is also harmful.

Creativity has a strong backbone in rationality. Sometimes creativity activates when primed with rational thought. Below you will see how rational principles can form and shape creative solutions.

While there are many principles under this category the most powerful and widely used are Grouping, Alignment, and Proportion. Grouping and Alignment are the two most important concepts you can understand. In almost every project, a pass at Grouping and Alignment can solve the majority of your design mistakes. These are two concepts you never want to forget.

GROUPING:

Design often starts as many fragmented pieces. Your job is to group those pieces into an aesthetic and valuable whole. When designing a house, for example, you must consider the interior (organizing rooms appropriately) in conjunction with the exterior (coordinating materials, windows and doors with the horizontal and vertical changes of the floorplan).

Frank Lloyd Wright provides us with an excellent example of how to group elements in his design of Falling Water, a house in Pennsylvania. Here you can see the exterior is simplified by using three material choices: stone, stucco, and glass. By doing this, he reduces the elements his mind needs to organize and can thus focus on refinement and creating a system that works.

Fallingwater
Photo by: Brian Donovan - https://www.flickr.com/photos/58621196@
N05/6134336955

Frank groups all horizontal elements in a stucco material. All vertical elements are made of stone, and glass is the glue that fills the gaps. These rules create a cohesive whole. You will notice that the glass is not "punched" in walls creating holes of light, but grouped in vertical and horizontal slivers of light. By simplifying and creating rules, he was able to make an creative and complex design from simple rules.

ALIGNMENT:

The home below is an excellent example of how windows can be Grouped and Aligned with architectural features.

Skylab architecture Skyline house.
Photo by: Skylab Architecture: http://www.designboom.com/architecture/skylab-architecture-skyline-residence/

The windows in the upper right corner are grouped together and aligned with the roof element. The windows in the center of the page align with the bottom of the second floor. The windows to the left align next to the vertical steel element that becomes the roof.

Most designs start with many variables, whether you are putting together a PowerPoint, organizing tasks, or placing windows on the exterior of a house. Taking another look at where you can group and align objects could do wonders for your project.

From a broader perspective, Alignment is about aligning the method, tools, and materials to the outcome you are targeting. If you are doing a creative project, does your process reflect your desired outcome? If you are creating a building that conveys strength, do your material choices reinforce that concept? If spending time with your family is important, does your calendar align with that goal?

PROPORTION:

Proportion is the size relationship between the elements in your design. The easiest way to understand Proportion is to relate it to nature and the human body. Vitruvius in his book *De Architecture* laid out the dimensions of a six-foot-tall man and used body parts to create different measurements. For example, the head is about 1/8 the size of the body. The torso is 3/8, and the legs are 4/8 of the body. You can use this concept when sketching people proportionally. If you mimic the proportions of nature, you can create a more intuitively pleasing design.

The notion of nature's aesthetic brings us to the golden ratio, a proportion that regularly appears in our natural environment. Architects have taken this ratio and applied it to spaces, buildings, and site layouts. The book *The Hidden Dimension* by Edward T. Hall offers an excellent example of using a grid and proportional overlay to designs. By overlaying the golden ratio over the Parthenon (seen on the next page), you can see the hidden system that helps guide its shape.

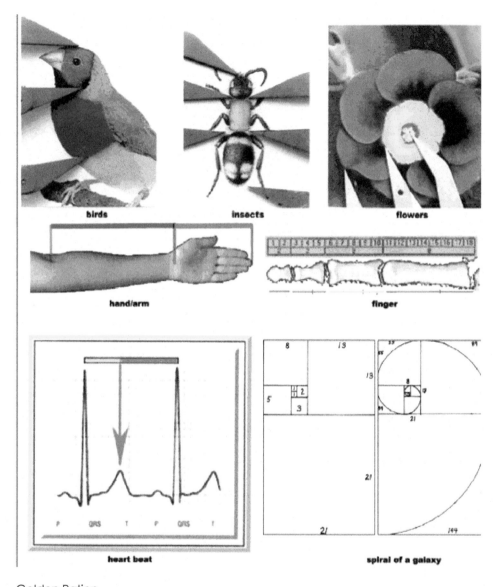

Golden Ration
Image by: J Richards: https://majorityrights.com/weblog/comments/the_facial_proportions_of_beautiful_people

The Parthenon
Image by: Jon R Childress: https://blog.johnrchildress.com/2011/05/13/magic-ratios/

The golden ratio can also be seen in modern structures. Below you can see it applied to the window configuration, and also the buildings massing.

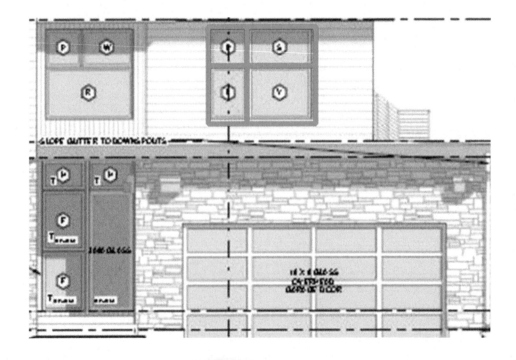

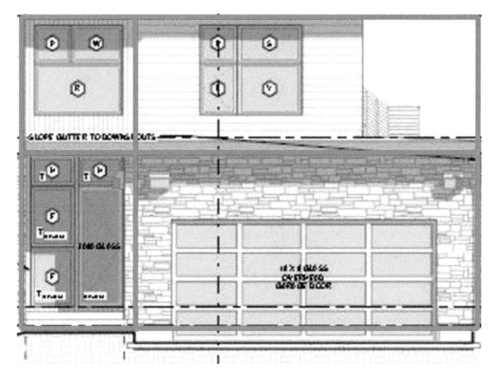

Goiden ratio in architecture
Image by: F9 Productions

By using the same proportions on different scales, we are mimicking the fractal process we see in nature itself. Fractals are a process of iteration, an operation that repeats over and over again. (7) The Fibonacci sequence generates the golden ratio. It is a relationship so special it has even been called "the Divine Proportion." (8)

We arrive at the Fibonacci sequence (0, 1, 1, 2, 3, 5, 8, 13) by adding the previous two numbers together to generate the next number in the sequence. For example:

$0 = 0$

$1 = 1$

$1 + 0 = 1$

$1 + 1 = 2$

$$1 + 2 = 3$$
$$2 + 3 = 5$$
$$3 + 5 = 8$$

The veins in your hand, the rivers of the world, to the roots and branches of a tree are all grown according to fractal laws. Fractals are nature's cheat sheet for creating complex things by repeating patterns. The simple equation recurs over and over again in an ongoing feedback loop. They are infinitely complex patterns that repeat on different scales to create unique results. In other words, rational thinking has a home in creative thought.

Our brain is hard-wired to see relationships and patterns. Recognizing them in our surroundings, even if only subconsciously, creates a pleasing feeling.

Proportion can be played with, teased, adjusted, and manipulated to arrive at the correct scale. Size and scale are elements of proportion. For example, if you are trying to convey a feeling of awe in your design, try including an oversized element. "Beefing up" the size of columns will communicate strength; slim supports will convey elegance. Think of a classic Greek government building vs. the Eiffel tower.

While proportions are about the physical relationship between elements, harmony is about the overall composition. It is about the relationship of people to spaces, spaces to structure, structure to materials, materials to the building, and the building to the historical and physical context. Harmony is how visual design elements relate, align, and complement each other to convey the unifying idea.

If the proportions or the materials you are using do not match the intent, it is akin to a choir member singing out of key. Your goal is to organize all the elements to sing the right tune. What you choose will come from your creative principles, and the success of that song will be determined by how well you execute with rational principles.

DESIGN EXAMPLE:

Here is a typical PowerPoint slide:

Regular Power Point Slides

- Point by point, points.
- No graphical relationship to the concept
- Stock image

http://www.publicdomainpictures.net/

How could we use the design principles we learned to create a more effective presentation?

1. If you are designing a PowerPoint, try changing the size and scale of your text to reflect the relative importance.
2. Relate the images or graphics to the feeling you are trying to convey.
3. Simplify the design to one concept per page.

Here is a PowerPoint example that uses these design principle:

As you can see, the text gives emotional power to the image. It lends this slide an intriguing feeling. The next slides' simplicity clearly conveys its message.

The "Goal Setting" text is set in the image, while the calendar image reinforces that goals are time-sensitive.

Hidden within this image is the alignment of the "Goal Setting" text with the iPad and keyboard. "Time Management" sits in the open space while the "T's" heel rests on the guideline.

While one regular PowerPoint slide could convey the same amount of information as the previous two combined, the designed slides deliver the message with far more emotion and engagement. Try redesigning a presentation you are working on using these principles.

Photoshop Tutorial Links are provided at:

alexandergore.com/bookresources

SUMMARY:

The rational thought process is often the key to implementing creative solutions. What we learned in this chapter is that it can also be the catalyst for new ideas. To throw out rational principles when trying to be creative would be like removing your car's steering wheel because you want to go where the road takes you. The creative and rational parts of your brain work hand in hand.

1. **Grouping**
   - Eliminate or reduce your design elements to three concepts.
   - Organize form with function.
   - Create rules. For example, a material change can only happen at physical changes.
2. **Alignment**
   - Alignment is about consistency.
   - Align aspects of your design, window, doors, deck, text, icons, etc. to each other.
   - Align the method, tools, and materials to the concepts, values, and the outcome you are targeting.
3. **Proportion**
   - Remember the Fibonacci sequence and golden ratio.
   - Use scale as emphasis.
   - Fractals are patterns repeated at different scales.

If creativity is about **Finding Connection through Contrast**, then rationality is about filling the **GAP** between imagination and creation. The GAP stands for **Grouping, Alignment, and Proportion**.

Harmony is your end goal. This is how visual design elements relate, align and complement each other to convey the unifying idea. It is where form meets function. To be effective, you must combine the creative and rational parts of your mind.

On the next page is a tool to help you advance on that goal. It is a circle set up in a yin and yang. Rationalization on the left, creativity on the right. The key is to limit what you are focusing on to produce the best result. Pick only three concepts to start your project. Then apply these principles not only to your design but to your process itself.

A design using flow, iteration, and symbolism might create a more natural form of architecture. Your process should reflect that. You might sketch 20 images before working on a computer. You might notate your drafts with ideas or relationships you are trying to instill in your design.

This filter is your starting guide. You will find new and different design principles as you evolve. Every time you start a design, take a look at this graphic and run a line through the concepts you are going to use. Think of each principle you choose as a filter to refine your design.

Run your thoughts through each of your selected principles to help you focus and polish your final product. The next chapter shows you examples of applying these principles to the creative process.

THE FILTER:

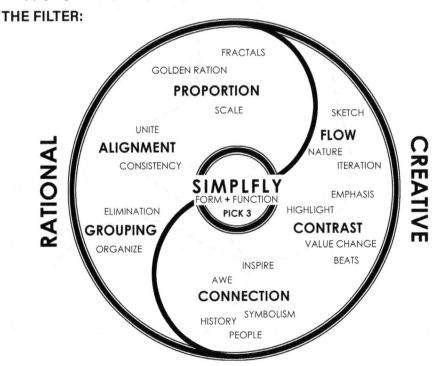

To print additional copies, visit alexandergore.com/bookresources.

The design Process.

If math is the universal language, then images and design are the universal translator. The Voyager satellite is Earths farthest spacecraft. Attached to the ship is a golden record. On the exterior of that record is our first attempt at contact with extraterrestrials. On there are not numbers, but diagrams and images designed to make communication with alien life possible. Let's dive into the design process. The process of creating images that convey emotions, and see how the visual part of our brain aids in creativity.

Ch. 3 | **THE DESIGN PROCESS**

We cannot solve our problems with the same thinking we used when we created them.

Albert Einstein

In this chapter, you will learn how to shape the system in which you operate. To be successful, we need to address the designer as well as the final product while designing. I believe this will not just be useful for those who design, but also for those who are interested in understanding themselves.

Most of us don't realize that design can change our lives. We live in cities where everything you see is the product of design, yet we rarely learn the process that created those designs. This chapter shapes the anvil that created the object.

At your job you might think you are only creating a report, inputting data, taking an order, moving merchandise, helping a customer, or reviewing a proposal, when in fact, something deeper is happening.

If you are creating a report you are selling an idea, either to a customer or your boss. Inputting data is creating order out of chaos. Moving merchandise is an exercise in organization and spatial design. I believe that learning the process of design can help you solve the processes ruling your life. Those who seek deeper meaning ask the most profound questions. They develop a superior understanding of solutions and advance faster. Design is not an exclusive tool for the creative class, but it is something everyone can use.

With today's technology, the ability to physically create your ideas has never been easier. Computer aided design programs are becoming ubiquitous. Funding is becoming more accessible via crowdsourcing, and 3D printing is becoming cheaper by the minute. **The products and ideas that will thrive in the future are those that not only fill a need, but are those with thoughtful, beautiful, and functional designs**. This chapter lays out the process designers use to make their projects successful.

Projects begin with a problem you are trying to solve, or a purpose you are aiming to achieve. This problem or purpose is filtered through a process whether you realize it or not. This filter is made up of your knowledge, the environment you are in, and the system you create. What that process looks like, and what tools you use shapes the outcome.

You might have heard the phrase, "If your only tool is a hammer then everything looks like a nail." Well, if you use the same process for a particular task, you will tend to produce similar results. For example, a freewheeling process could lead to unique solutions, but it could also risk a late delivery, being over budget, and even inconsistent results. On the other hand, a rigid process could lead solutions that are done on time and under budget but are utterly dull.

A design problem could be drafting a building plan, a poster, a marketing campaign, a dating strategy, or outlining how to grow your business.

For example, designing a building usually involves balancing a variety of items: the program (rooms, sizes, requirements), the client's desires, building codes, construction cost, materials, etc. How all these parts come together becomes part of the design process.

A design problem has many undefined factors. Thus, when trying to solve design problems, you must start with its process. Often many fail, not because they are incompetent, but because they do not take the time to design the process before designing the product. You must make an anvil before creating a sword. Most of us fall short by banging steel against a rock and wonder why our sword comes out looking like a crooked wand. Knowing the design process can help you create better solutions.

It's easy to get stuck traveling too fast down the wrong road. To correct this, we must make a design process map that can help us refine our ideas.

INVESTIGATE:

My only genius talent is inquisitiveness.
Albert Einstein

A | ASK THE RIGHT QUESTIONS.

The most important thing you can do when you start a project is to spend time making sure you're solving the correct problem. People can spend weeks, months or even years going down the wrong path.

For example, I have seen millions of dollars spent designing and constructing homes that are oriented incorrectly on the site. Land in Colorado is expensive. One major reason for that expense is the incredible view of the Rocky Mountains. The house on the left on the next page oriented itself towards the street by default. The gorgeous views of the Rocky Mountains and Longs Peak, one of the most picturesque mountains in America is to the southwest. This home consciously (or unconsciously) gave that view to the corner of the garage.

In the image on the right, on the next page, you can see a house a couple of hundred feet away from the first home. A significant portion of their home is orientated to take advantage of the amazing views on their lot.

By simply mirroring the home on the left, or by using a different design

Image from: Google Earth, edited by Alex Gore.

they could have taken advantage of the views they paid a premium to have.

As a designer, you have to ask yourself constantly: what is the real problem or opportunity? Whatever the problem, don't just solve the symptoms but instead search for the root of the issue. If there's an opportunity, ask how you can take advantage of it. Start by asking the

> Experience often deeply embeds the assumptions
> that you need to question in the first place.

Chris Sacca on Tim Ferriss podcast (10)

fundamental questions.

Let's say you were starting a business for the first time. How would you go about it? Business school or common sense might teach you to find the best location, hire an accountant, estimate all of your expenses and income, hire a lawyer to create your contracts, and start trying to get business right away. Doing all those things sounds like the best way to approach starting a business. But ask yourself what are you truly solving? In that scenario, you are only addressing the problem of how to design your business. You are not spending time on how to solve your clients' problems.

Lance and my business origin story is quite different from the typical approach. I was laid off in early 2009. I called Lance and told him I was going back to school for a year to earn my Master's Degree in Construction Management. Hopefully, by the time I graduated the recession would be over.

We kept talking over the next several months, and I started listening to a podcast by a guy named Pat Flynn who was talking about how to create multiple streams of income. I mentioned this idea to Lance, who immediately said he could start making BIM models (these are computer models of the built environment) and sell them. I said, great, and I'll start building a website.

In late 2009 Lance was then laid off and had to find work on his own. Through the BIM models, he landed a huge client who wanted him to do that sort of modeling on a consistent and paid basis. He also then began to land some architecture work. I joined him in May of 2010, and started landing work also. We immediately knew that the market for large and high-priced homes was at a standstill, so we only concentrated on the small additions market. We made the decision that we would target a slew of smaller jobs to make up for the larger projects that no longer existed. Our idea was, "profit and success through volume."

At this point, the country was deep in the recession, and the construction industry was a dog eat dog world. Lance had a wife and kids to support, and I refused to live in my parents' house any longer.

To get a feel of the market, we created a Craigslist ad for a small house to locate the market. We advertised as a client who was looking for an architect/draftsman to draw up a cabin. From there we gained the pricing and contracts of our competitors.

We knew we couldn't compete with the moonlighters who were doing design work after their workday, and had the lowest fees. But we also couldn't offer the same service of the higher priced big firms. So we positioned ourselves in the middle of the pack.

We also noticed that the contracts we received varied wildly. Some would be a one or two sentence email response with a price. Others would be a full five-page contract with a lot of legal boilerplates. We decided to reexamine our contract through the lens of the client. We asked the question, "If I were the client, what would I like to see in the contract?"

What resulted was a contract that broke the job down into a week by week calendar, showing what we would deliver and how much each phase would cost. While you might think this would be common sense, I think you would be surprised to know that it is not standard practice.

Lastly, we created a template and a system so that we could handle a large volume of work at a professional level. Because of this high volume of work, we were able to gain experience and competence at a quicker pace than our peers while at the same time surviving the great recession.

To recap, we asked simple questions:

Where is the market?
What would a client want to see in a contract?
How can we deliver what they want in a fast and professional manner?

In this way, we designed the business around the clients' needs. We solved the real problem, rather than spinning our wheels by constantly revising a business plan that had no basis in reality. The result was that from 2009 to 2015 we were able to grow our firm from $0.00 to $500,000.00 in annual revenue, and from two people to a six-person firm.

The speculative BIM models Lance started making in 2010 and the template we have refined over five years have become the content we sell and case studies share at www.RevitFurniture.com.

Everyone has to start somewhere. Before we let our students design, we assign them a case study of a bridge or a house. They are required to write a three-page report that investigates the following: the environment, user behaviors, form, function, utility, and details.

We do this for a couple of reasons. 1) Start by standing on the shoulders of giants. Use the best examples to start at a higher level than you could by yourself. 2) Case studies can help you focus and boil down what others have done to create a solution. You can use these examples to find first principles or to start designing by analogy.

Investigation is the crux of creativity. It about spending the time to find the actual problem you are trying to solve. By using your understanding of the problem, and asking deeper questions you can converge on the best solution. Great leaders ask great questions.

B | ANALOGY VS. FIRST PRINCIPLES

To understand creativity, you must know how you think when you are creating. The first thing you need to recognize is whether you can solve your problem by analogy or by first principles. Solving by analogy is comparing what you want to do, with what has been done before. Solving by first principles means boiling down a problem to its fundamental truths, and reasoning up from there. Understanding the difference between these two thought patterns, and how to use them, can release untapped creativity.

Let's say you are building a house in a neighborhood. The existing homes often have a similar style, use the same materials, and are of comparable size. Solving the problem by analogy means designing your new home to match the existing homes in the area.

The benefit of this way of thinking is uniformity. Your house will be cost competitive you are using similar materials that are readily available on the market. It will be built quicker because the carpenters will be familiar with the system for assembling your home. And you will have a connection to the neighborhood and its inhabitants by sharing a similar aesthetic.

Now let's examine this same problem by using first principle thinking. Let's say you wanted to build a house in the same neighborhood as before.

In this case, you wouldn't try to mimic your neighbors. You would start by asking what is this house for and what is it supposed to do for me? One conclusion you could come up with would be to sustain you and your family.

Sustainability is the ability of a system to endure. Currently, the construction industry uses a LEED certification (Leadership in Energy and Environmental Design), or a HERS rating (Home Energy Rating System) to determine a home's sustainability level. These are regulated verification programs that determine your home's level of sustainability on a point scale. These are complicated programs that involves checklist, forms, and fees. It frequently results in a building that uses less harmful chemicals and more energy efficient.

The criticism of these programs is they don't address the essential aspect of sustainability. They are creating buildings whose goal is to waste energy less than the average home. If they can't achieve that, the solution is to slap solar panels on the design to create green energy. While they are gaining great press, the system is more insulated than integrated. The Spanish word *insolar* expresses what the green rating systems actually do best. "Insolar" happens to be the same word for insulate and isolate. What we are doing today is isolating ourselves from the natural environment and others by insulation. To me, this doesn't strike at the true nature of sustainability.

So instead of meddling through that mess, which would be designing from analogy, you would use first principles. Ask yourself what does it mean to be sustainable? Could this home help me survive if the power went off? Does it help sustain the fundamental elements of life (e.g. food, water, heat, and shelter)? Does it eliminate waste and toxic chemicals?

The rules you would create for that home might look like this.

1. Use natural materials such as wood, stone, metal, glass, straw bale,

or rammed earth.

2. Orient the longest part of your building south, place most of your windows and stone on that side and shade appropriately. Doing so allows you to take advantage of the sun's free heat in the winter, and block it in the summer with roof overhangs.

3. Strawbale walls are excellent sustainable insulation. The north side of the building is an excellent location for such a wall.

4. Design in 2' increments. Most products come in 2' increments, so this will eliminate waste.

5. Collect rainwater from your roof. But be aware of your local laws. In some states this is illegal.

6. Have a garden for food and chickens for eggs.

7. Compost your leftovers to create soil for your garden.

8. Insulate well. Don't lose the heat you already captured or created.

9. Think about using alternative energy such as solar panels or geothermal.

   Most solar systems today feed right into the grid and shut down with the grid. You will need to have your system designed so that it will work in case the power goes out.

10. Don't forget to bring life indoors. You can have a indoor kitchen garden for parsley, cilantro, rosemary and other small foods. You can clean and provide fresh air for your home. Design with these spaces in mind.

Kamal Meattle is the CEO of the Paharpur Business Center & Software Technology Incubator Park in New Delhi, India. He had a hard time breathing the polluted air and found a surprisingly simple solution. He figured out that by using three plants he can completely clean and create oxygen to keep his building fresh. The prescription is to:

Use four shoulder-height Areca Palms per person to convert CO_2 to oxygen during the day. Use 6-8 waist-high Mother-in-law's Tongue to convert CO_2 to oxygen during the night. Lastly, add Money Plants to remove toxins.

You can see his talk here:

http://www.ted.com/talks/kamal_meattle_on_how_to_grow_your_own_fresh_air

Thinking from first principles allows you to solve the problem as you see fit, rather than relying on systems others have built. In Part II of this book, you will see how you can reconsider everything from a chicken coop to a skyscraper through these lenses.

I have been designing through first principles since college. I didn't know that there was a term for this way of thinking until recently. I first heard of this term "first principles" in a video where Elon Musk explained this way of thinking. He is a huge proponent of thinking from first principles. For more about his thought process check out this link: http://jamesclear.com/first-principles.

C | CREATE YOUR ANVIL

In design, we commonly call the inspirational idea or organizing force the "Parti." This initial organizing idea is the end goal of the investigation process.

Let's take the fundamental starting point, nature, and see if it can give us some hints to its million plus years of success. By exploring and investigating a simple picture or scene, we can start to extrapolate ideas that we can apply to our built world. Nature often has a silent soul that we all yearn to understand.

Take for example the picture below. What thoughts or ideas can you

Nature image
Photo by: Joel Bedford - https://www.flickr.com/photos/jalex_photo/1525171367

take from this image that might inform a building design? Take a minute and think of two ideas before moving on.

One of the first ideas I take from this photo is how trees naturally diffuse light, creating filtered shadows. What if our awnings, windows, or even roofs mimicked this property? I can see rooms bathed in filtered golden light from skylights above, resembling the natural filter created by trees in nature. The natural sunlight also highlights the gradual color of the rock and the different hues of the vegetation. Quality natural lighting and soft colors can be a great inspiration for designers.

The second idea that comes to mind is the sense of touch. This picture makes me want to pick up the rocks and toss small stones into the standing water. I want to feel my feet on the hard rock, and in the fresh water. How can we bring this sensation into our buildings? Maybe we can't afford to place stone everywhere, but could we place it in a space where one can pause and reflect? Maybe the entrance, the mirrored bathroom wall, or my personal favorite, placing brick behind the head of the bed. These are all great spaces for personal reflection.

The last idea that comes to mind from this image is the sense of wonder and exploration. Malls and casinos take advantage of this feeling of exploration. They will place an attractive property just around the bend. For malls, it would be the big box stores such as JC Penney, Best Buy, etc.

In casinos, it might be an exciting new game just around the corner. They place something, in sight but out of reach. This way you see a hint of what is to come, and you are invited to go further to explore. Developers put interesting items on the far sides of the development so you will have to walk past everything else they have to offer before getting there. Malls and resorts are also mimicing nature by using stone, placing in water falls and introducing plants.

As shown, nature can provide a large variety of ideas, but these examples barely scrape the surface of all the secrets nature has to offer us in design. Whenever you start a project first familiarize yourself with what already exists, then reduce what you are investigating to elements that apply to your project. This investigation can either inspire you to build on previous progress or show you of what not to do. This step sets the standard and tone for your project. Whatever you are doing, study the best examples. Choose the best: buildings, business plans, processes, ideas, or concepts. Investigate what is working and what is not.

Take visual notes that you can come back to later for inspiration if you are stuck. By processing information in a novel way, unique results can happen. For example, Zaha Hadid starts most designs by painting, Steven Holl by water coloring. Use sketching and drawing to give you insights others won't have. Learn how to draw and take visual notes in the appendix.

Q: How can an example help you find clarity in a current project?

The key when analyzing cases is to try to understand the process or rules behind the decisions they made. This way you won't be designing only from analogy. You will start to understand the first principles they began with and can either apply or discard those thoughts in your project.

Below are some places to start looking for examples.

DESIGN STUDENTS:

Houses: Lake Flato, Jonathan Segal, Olson Kundig
Buildings: BIG Architects, Norman Foster, Steven Holl

BUSINESS STUDENTS: (Hint we are all business students.)

How can nature inspire you to refine your process?
How can design principles inform your projects?

PROTIP: Read Walter Isaacson's book: Steve Jobs.

There is often pushback of the idea of following other peoples example because we don't want to copy them. We want our life. We are looking for a breakthrough, to be better, to be different! But learning from others doesn't mean you have to copy them. Steve Jobs learned from his mechanically inclined father that it was beneficial to know what every part costs, and how to obtain the best price. When Steve was learning from his Dad, was he studying to become a mechanic? No, he took the ideas that worked and applied them to his life, and Apple became one of the most profitable companies in history because of this mindset.

Jobs understood the principle and applied it to his situation. The same idea executed by different people can lead to completely different products, businesses, and results. So begin with the best, dissect examples to learn the levers you can pull, and find what works for you.

REDUCE: USE SIMPLE INGREDIENTS

Nature builds complexity from simplicity. Time, gravity, and water are all that was needed to create the Grand Canyon. We can learn from nature that simplicity can create amazing complex things. In the Rational Principles chapter, we saw how the Fibonacci's sequence, adding the last two numbers together to get the next number in the sequence, creates the golden ratio, the divine proportion of nature.

SIDE NOTE | Gordon Ramsay, a famous chef, often prescribed three solutions to turn a restaurant around in his show "Kitchen Nightmares": 1) Reduce the menu, 2) Use better ingredients, and 3) Redesign the dining room and the kitchen.

In architecture, a good reason for simplification is so that you can focus more on the problem. Simplicity keeps you from getting caught up in juggling too many variables. By following the simple rule of limiting the materials you use to three or less, you can focus and be less distracted. You will be able to dive into the essence of a project. Move to a deeper understanding of the problem, and ultimately come up with a better solution.

For example, many of the world's most famous buildings limit the amount of materials they use. The Sydney Opera House is dominated by one primary material—its concrete shell. The Eiffel Tower's only dominant material is iron. The key is reduction, which leads to a determined focus. Clarity follows, arriving at a solution that solves the problem on a deeper level.

The architect Tadao Ando showcases this concept brilliantly. He creates amazing buildings by mainly focusing on one material: concrete. He is an expert in this medium. Thus his buildings can become more

Sydney Opera House
Photo by: Hai Linh Truong - http://discoverdreamland.blogspot.com/2011/03/
wonderful-places-to-visit.html

Photo from Library of Congress Author unknown. : http://loc.gov/pictures/
resource/cph.3f03714/

Tadao Ando - Church of Light
Photo by: Yale Breslin - http://lifeandtimes.com/the-architecture-of-concrete

nuanced and sophisticated than others because of his understanding. His self-imposed limitation essentially becomes liberating because he can do much more with concrete than anyone else can.

After teaching our students at the University of Colorado sketching, design principals, and the computer program they will use, we give them a design project. In the project, we tell our students to limit their exterior to three materials. Glass is a requirement, leaving them only two more to select.

PROTIP: Whatever you are doing, try eliminating multiple variables. More variables often obscure your understanding the root problem. You'll want to start with the basics. Ask simple questions that need answering. Focus on fundamentals and build a strong foundation.

ITERATE, ITERATE, ITERATE:

Once you have found some examples and narrowed your focus, you can become flexible in looking for solutions. A key design concept is iterations. I cannot overstate the importance of this step. You have probably heard of the phrase: "practice makes perfect." Well, iterations are practice. You wouldn't expect to throw a football once and be a great quarterback. Why then would one design make you a great designer? Everytime I produce a rendering I learn a new skill or trick.

Iterations can be segmented. Take for example a typical football practice. There is usually a warm up, individual position drills, group offense and defense walkthroughs, a scrimmage, and conditioning. Each phase emphasizes repetition. Repetition is practice and practice makes perfect.

In design, you can "warm up" by browsing magazines or the Internet for examples. You can perform individual drills by sketching nature and concepts. "Walkthroughs" are discussions about ideas with your friends. Scrimmaging is designing, and conditioning is the realization that it might take 10, 15, 100 tries to get a design that works.

Design thinking places a heavy emphasis on refinement. Many other disciplines do too; the significant differences are that the tools you are using are visual, and the result is usually physical. As you improve, you might arrive at a solution more quickly. You might also notice you sketch eight concepts, and the first one was the best. Doing so is usually the result of your intuition at work. If this happens, look at your sketches and ask yourself, why did the first one work more than the others? That way you will start to understand your intuition better and use it on command.

In your iterations, you can switch between using rational principles, and engaging your creative subconscious.

EVALUATE:

In between iterations you can use the principles of design that you used to create your object to evaluate what you have created. Re-examine what you have created so you can improve. Your assessment might mean realigning spaces, redesigning the exterior, or refining every piece so it becomes part of a seamless whole. This iterate/evaluate process can happen multiple times.

The most important, and unique aspect of architecture school was the constant presence of the critique. The critique differs from a presentation in that students must present to a panel that provides feedback rather than an audience. Students have to present their ideas visually with drawings, renderings, and models about twice a semester while being able to explain the project effectively.

Normally your project would have two major critiques, the midpoint and the final. In between these critiques were "desk crits." The professor would come to your desk at least once a week to analysze and help you refine your project.

Later in the book, we will create a checklist to evaluate your project at key points. The lesson here is to not only use design tools when shaping your end product but to use them to develop your process.

SUMMARY |

INVESTIGATE:

Investigation is the key to creativity. You can remember the A,B,C's of investigate this way. "**A**" stands for the first letter in the phrase "Ask Good Questions." "**B**" stands for beta test which generally means testing two items against eachother. Which relates to either Analogy or First Principle thinking. Lastly "**C**" stands for the first letter in the phase "Create the Anvil."

A| Ask good questions

Find great examples.

Ask great questions to create great results.

What are your opportunities?

B| Analogy vs First Principles

Are you repeating something that has been done. Use Analogy

Are you trying something new. Boil the problem down to its fundamental principles and ration up from there.

C| Create your Anvil

Hint: Let the environment guide you.

What are you trying to solve?

REDUCE:

Use the best ingredient (materials, tools, programs, teachers).

Create your filter from the Design Principles chapter.

What is your parti?

ITERATE:

Use design principles (Rational).

Grouping, Alignment, Consistency, and Contrast

Engage your subconscious (Creative).

Flow, Connection, and Contrast

Sketch, hone your skills.

EVALUATE:

INVESTIGATE

- ASK GREAT QUESTIONS
- ANALOGY OR FIRST PRINCIPLE?
- CREATE YOUR ANVIL

REDUCE

- USE THE BEST INGREDIENTS
- REDUCE TO 3 OR LESS

ITERATE

- USE RATIONAL PRINCIPLES
- ENGAGE THE CREATIVE
  SUBCONSCIOUS
- HONE YOUR SKILLS

EVALUATE

-FINALIZE A UNIFYING CONCEPT OR PARTI.
- HOLD YOURSELF ACCOUNTABLE.
- -DO YOUR ELEMENTS REINFORCE YOUR CONCEPT?

Finalize a unifying concept or parti.

Hold yourself accountable.

Do your elements reinforce your concept?

This process is a framework for finding the right question to answer, not the right solution. The successfulness of your solutions is related to the power of your questions. Whatever your field—business, science, marketing, healthcare, etc.—the design process is the x-ray lens that will help you find a better solution. It is a visual exploration of a problem. It taps into the natural way we learn and can enable us to communicate with more clarity.

The next section will provide insight into the tools and processes we just learned by walking you through real-life examples. These examples will lay the concepts bare for you to examine, pick apart and learn from what worked and what could work better. They will also detail the personal struggles that come with trying to find elegant solutions to common

PART 2
DESIGN

DESIGN PREFACE | AN EXTREMELY BRIEF HISTORY OF ARCHITECTURE

In *The Architecture of Happiness*, Alain de Botton lays out how architecture reflected the technical skills and ability of a society to exploit its natural resources. For example, only large societies could use materials that were not in its immediate surroundings. Thus style was only able to change when either transportation or technology allowed. In the modern United States transportation has been solved to such an extent that materials are ubiquitous across thousands of miles. That is why a neighborhood in Georgia can look strikingly similar to a neighborhood in Salt Lake City.

One of the most important ideas in the modern era of architecture was that a building was a reflection of the person who created it. Louis

Sullivan, the father of skyscrapers and mentor to Frank Lloyd Wright, thought of buildings as a mirror into the soul of the designer. There's no hiding who you are in your designs. By learning how to design, we can see a window into our own soul.

Louis Khan was famous for the phrase that he would ask a brick what it wanted to be and would listen to it. This idea harkens to listing and using materials in their pure form. In the Phillips Exeter Library, he separates the uses of materials to coincide with their natural properties. He used concrete as the structure because of its naturally strong yet fluid properties. He used wood to line the book stacks so that people could enjoy its natural, inviting warmth.

The genius designer Buckminster Fuller thought of the earth as a spaceship floating around the sun and his perspective transformed the way we look at the world. He asked the famous architect Norman Foster "How much does your building weigh?" This question led Norman to think about architecture more akin to shipbuilding, or as a product. These ideas are being advanced by Bjarke Ingles of BIG, an architecture firm that is pushing the limits of sustainability and design.

I believe we are now entering a new phase of architecture where we blend old ideas with new technology. **If Kahn asked the brick what it wants to be, let's now ask the brick what it wants to do**. In doing so, we are connecting to our sustainable roots while reflecting our technologically driven society—one where phones, computers, cars and trains perform tasks for us. Let's demand the same of our architecture, and not just the objects we put in them. Let's ask a roof to collect water, not to just shed it. Let's ask walls to store heat, not to just block the outdoor environment. Let's not look at aesthetics as cake decoration, but as something that reflects the true soul of the buildings.

The preceding chapter combines the principles and processes we learned in the first chapters with the idea that architecture isn't something that just is, but something that can do.

The
Roost

4

Here you see the beginings of a pattern in design and thought. A fractal if you will, that repeats on a grander scale. Where can this thinking take you.. only the imagination can tell.

Ch. 4 | **THE ROOST**

Creativity is just connecting things. When you ask creative people how they did something, they feel a little guilty because they didn't really do it, they just saw something. It seemed obvious to them after a while. That's because they were able to connect experiences they've had and synthesize new things. And the reason they were able to do that was that they've had more experiences than other people.

Steve Jobs

I believe most of you are like me. You see things the way they are and ask why. The answer, no matter if it is work, home or politics normally is that it has been that way so long you can't change it. But what if you could? This section is about small changes in small steps.

Most things you create are for someone else. Your work is mostly your for employers, or for your teachers if you are in school. The Roost was a chance to build something my way.

I could have bought a chicken coop, but I didn't like what I saw on the market. There was also an idea in me that had to become physical. I wanted to design something that flowed with nature. I wanted a structure that communed with its environment. Rain would be its lifeblood running throughout the structure. The breeze would be its breath. The sun its substance.

INVESTIGATION:

When looking at examples of henhouses for my chickens I came across the unassailable fact that chickens must love traditional craftsman architecture. It surprised me that chickens from Alabama to Seattle loved the same type of design. What was even more perplexing is how they communicate their preference to us. I couldn't help but wonder: why do they love craftsman architecture so much?

Traditional Chicken Coop:
Photo by: Kaiya Cayko

Since we have yet to break the chicken to human communication barrier, I decided the existing examples would not be of any help me. So I then began to investigate the problems that needed solving. Chickens need:

1. Shelter from the environment
2. A safe place to lay their eggs
3. Water to drink
4. Food to eat
5. Heat when it's cold and a cool breeze when it is warm.

To me, the conventional store-bought chicken coops only solve: providing shelter and a place to lay their eggs. They leave the rest for humans to do as daily chores. Imagine if design could solve all of these problems without human interference.

I believe the solution to a self-sustaining chicken coop is to utilize nature's resources. The sky brings drinking water in the form of rain. The wind blows a cool breeze in the summer. The sun and the chickens' body heat radiate warmth in the winter. Finally, by combining the sun with the rain and seeds, lettuce is grown to help feed the chickens. The chickens provide eggs for me, and their waste converts into compost over the winter for use in the garden next spring — which then gets used for planting lettuce for them to eat.

But the question remained: how can you combine these forces with the architecture? Traditional chicken coops, and sadly some homes, are constructed from the lowest quality, and most widely available products. The key to solving this problem, and many others, is discarding standard solutions. Instead of using an asphalt shingled roof, and wood/vinyl siding we can use better materials that solve multiple problems at one time.

The metal roof can do more than keep the coop dry. It sheds rainwater into a collection system, separating it for the chickens to drink, and to water the plants. The water naturally circulates itself, being replenished by new rain. The excess water drains through a hose to a planter in the coop, and to the garden outside to grow lettuce. The chickens eat the lettuce and produce eggs for my family and me, which completes the cycle.

COOP **LIFE CYCLE**

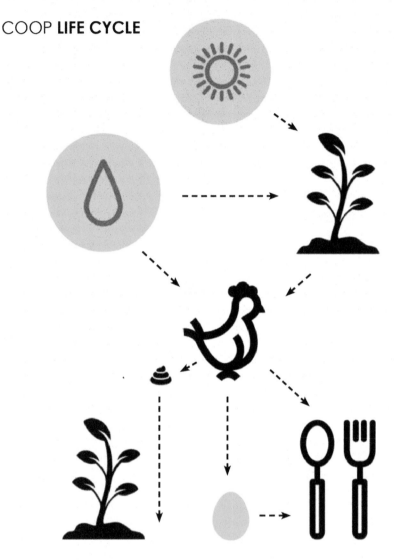

1) Sun + Water makes plants grow

2) Plants + Water = food for the chickens

3) Chickens and eggs = food for us

4) Chicken waste can be added to the compost inorder to make soil for the plants grow in.

Photos by: Alex Gore

The deep roof overhangs shade the stone in the summer, reflecting heat and keeping the coop cool. In the winter, when the sun is low, the stone absorbs the heat during the day. At night when the temperature cools, the stones release their stored heat to warm the coop.

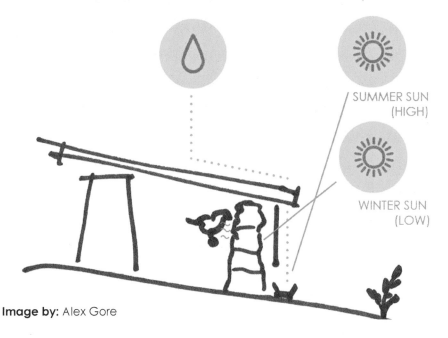

SUMMER SUN
(HIGH)

WINTER SUN
(LOW)

Image by: Alex Gore

Photos by: Alex Gore

The chickens perch on a rod near the stone wall, allowing them to keep warm. Plexiglass placed on the exterior prevents the heat from escaping. On the north side of the chicken coop, I opted to use a strawbale wall instead of using wood. The straw wall has a high natural insulation value of R-27.5 / 19 inches of thickness, and it retains heat very well. (11)

"R" is a material's ability to resist temperature transfer. Thus keeping

Photos by: Alex Gore

in the heat provided by the sun and the chicken's body temperature for longer periods of time. Vents on the top of the east and west walls can be removed in the summer to allow cooling air to pass through the building and sweep out the hot air.

The two-part door is also used to control the temperature. During the summer the large door is left open to let the breeze in (Door 1). During the winter a smaller door is used to protect the inside from the harsh temperatures outside (Door 2). The CMU (Concrete Masonry Unit) at the bottom of the door serves as a step for the chickens during the day. At night it is propped up as a deterrent to keep raccoons prying hands from trying to open the doors. I have had to run out in the middle of the night and protect the chickens from up to three raccoons at a time trying to get in and eat them. Luckily they have never breached the coop. By using appropriate materials, and simple passive design strategies, the chicken coop can regulate its temperature—and protect its residents—much better than traditional structures.

The coop is stacked on two CMU blocks at each of the four corners. They keep the wood base off the ground, thus preserving it from moisture.

Photo by: Alex Gore

The elevated foundation also provides outdoor shade in the summer. The chickens have now decided this is the perfect place to lay their eggs, making me crawl under the coop to retrieve my breakfast.

In exchange for the chickens' eggs, you need to feed, water, protect them from the environment, and keep them warm. Most coops only protect chickens from the wind and rain.

By using design principles, architecture can start to do more than be just an idle box flashed with fancy styles; it can help sustain itself. It can interact, contribute, and weave itself with the environment and society. In the next chapters, we will see how these design principles can reshape everything from houses to skyscrapers.

SUMMARY | Design Steps

1: Think deeper.

Investigate the actual problem you are trying to solve. In this case, you are not trying to just house chickens; you are creating a system to help them live. By re-examining the problem, and not accepting standard solutions, you can create new opportunities.

2: Use design principles to align opportunities with solutions.

A roof not only sheds rain but also provides water for drinking and growing plants. The sun heats the building by harnessing the natural properties of the stone.

3: Sketch

Your brain engages its visual IQ by sketching. It can combine different ideas in unique and innovating combinations.

4: Start

A chicken coop is a small step. Insignificant in the scheme of things, but it creates momentum. Something you can build upon.

Atlas

5

Don't be satisfied with the options given to you. You can create your own solutions, your own world. The world tries to make you choose between Pepsi and Coke, Republican and Democrat. This is a false choice, take life into your own hands.

Be the change you want to see in the world.

Mahatma Gandhi

While on vacation with friends, I sat alongside a beautiful stream just outside Glacier National Park when the rain rolled in. A group of us went inside the RV and started playing cards. After about an hour it dawned on me that we had locked ourselves inside a plastic box, with small windows completely cut off from one of the most gorgeous places in the world. I don't make it to national parks often, and here I was hanging out inside, instead of enjoying the great outdoors.

A couple of years after that experience another group of friends and myself were camping by a lake in Colorado. While we were outside fishing, hiking, and making food by the campfire, I noticed the family slightly downhill from our campground rarely left their RV. I could hear the growl of their generator pumping electricity to their running air conditioning unit. Sometimes the screen door would creak open, only to be slammed shut moments later.

One small window punctuated the exterior on each side. Surrounding the RV was beautiful brown bark lying on the ground. The green tree canopy swayed in the breeze, and a blue hue coming off the lake in the distance blended seamlessly into the sky. Smack dab in the middle of the scene was a dirty 1990's RV that looked like a love child conceived between "Mad Max" and your local trailer park.

I knew there had to be a better solution. Can we design a structure that is mobile, but also lets people connect with nature? Can you be inside without disconnecting from the outdoors? RV's offer great mobility, and tiny homes (a new lifestyle movement—Google it, if you are unaware, but be ready to fall down a rabbit hole) offer exceptional craftsmanship. Can these two concepts be blended? Too often we are disconnected from the stunning places we live. The solution we devised was Atlas which seeks to reconnect us with our environment.

Tiny homes often mimic the traditional pitched roof shape of a house. They use quality wood material, which is often heavy. It makes them hard to tow and not very aerodynamic. RV's are lightweight, and more aerodynamic, but even upscale options provide an interior aesthetic that feels fake and out of place with stunning natural landscapes. Somehow marble countertop with vinyl floors doesn't mix well in a mobile structure set in the forest.

By combining the best quality of each industry, we designed a hybrid solution that meets the aerodynamic demands while allowing more of natural world inside. By letting the environment be our guide, we can start to mold our design.

Photo by: Guillaume Dutilh - Tiny House Giant Journey

Photo by: Alex Gore

Most people start the design process focused on the floor plan. For obvious reasons, we began with the shape. Instead of taking on the pitched roof commonly seen in the tiny house community, we opt for a one-way sloped roof to provide an aerodynamic frame. This slope serves as a mounting point for solar panels, and a collection plane for rain.

To see where to focus next, we need to find where the problem takes us. The issue with campers and RV's is that they are not well connected with the outdoors. Thesolution doesn't lie in the design of the floor plan, but rather the design of the walls. Coming up with unique solutions often requires a unique process.

Instead of seeing a wall as mostly solid with punched windows, Atlas' reverses the notion. One entire side is glass, with multiple measures in place to protect it. Atlas is engineered from scratch to eliminate waste and enhance optimal performance while remaining elegant. A steel frame encompasses the entire structure, surrounding the glass stabilizing it from violent forces.

Photo by: Anni Gore

A deck hinges off the frame. When it's time to hit the road, the deck folds up and nests into the frame to protect the glass. When stationary, the deck folds down to provide an outdoor living area. Retractable legs are lowered to land softly on the ground.

Photo by: McCall Burau

Photo by: McCall Burau

An awning lifts up from the protective frame to provide shade through its perforated aluminum skin. Its shape is the reverse of the slope of the roof and, accordingly, the angle of the deck. The deck's shape puts the largest area near the entrance, creating space for the bigger hinge. The smaller hinge near the rear of the house supports the smaller area of the deck. The awning mirrors this slope, providing shade over the bar and the highest portion of the glass.

PRO TIP: At this point, the design resembles a half-complete puzzle. As more pieces get put in place, the remaining ones become easier and quicker to assemble. Creativity is like solving a puzzle where you don't have a picture as a guide. Most people get lost, putting together pieces that don't fit just because they are near or easy to grab. The key to success is creating a compelling image in your mind of the final result—a picture that solves the problem—then developing a filter to find the right pieces that fit your image.

After Atlas's form, glass wall, and deck have been put in place, the floor plan can take shape. A natural location for the kitchen is over the wheel wells, as the cabinetry will hide the wheels wells. Placed over the countertop are three windows that open to create a bar connecting the indoors with the outdoor deck. They allow for easy passing of food and drink. They also let fresh air inside.

Opposite the kitchen are the stairs and storage to cover the other wheel well, which balances out the weight of the window walls. This allowed the trailer to be lower and the space inside to be higher. Atlas also uses light gauge steel instead of traditional wood framing to lower the total weight. Light gauge steel is about ⅓ the weight of wood.

Full stairs create a homier feel than the ship ladder typically seen in these small spaces. Under the stairs is storage space for clothes, boots, and board games. Doors glides out, keeping in line with the transformer idea of the whole project. The stair landing acts as a desk for work. At the top of the stairs is a bed with more storage. At the base of the stairs is a futon that can fold out to accommodate more guests.

Photo by: McCall Burau

FIRST FLOOR:

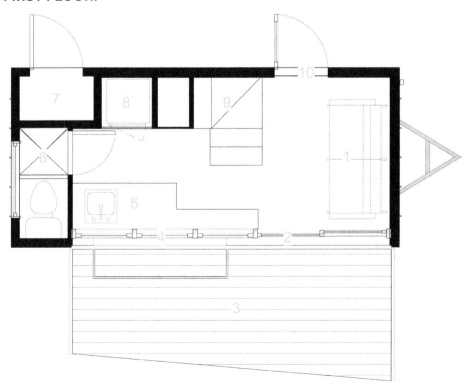

1. Fold out futon (Sleeps two)
2. Sliding glass door
3. Deck
4. Operable windows for inside/outside bar
5. Kitchen
6. Shower and toilet
7. Storage, solar batteries, backup generator
8. Refrigerator and pantry
9. Stairs with built-in storage
10. Glass door with opener and thumb-lock.

UPPER FLOOR:

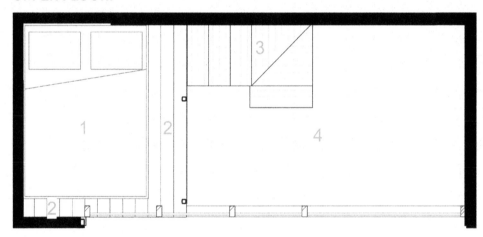

1. Queen size bed (Sleeps two)
2. Loft storage
3. Stairs
4. Open to below

As for materials, we don't believe in laminate floors, composite materials, plastic or vinyl for this design. Especially in a design meant for the parks and most beautiful spaces in our world. There are enough fake things out there already, and we do not need to contribute. We believe in truth in material and truth in design. Accordingly, the majority of Atlas is made up of three main materials: Metal, Glass, and Wood. Every inch was designed with a purpose, and that purpose was to connect people with nature.

MATERIALS:

1. Tube steel creates a strong frame around the entire house and the window wall. Light gauge steel is used in between to reduce weight.

2. Wood for a natural feel and smooth, warm finish.

3. Glass to fully experience your surroundings.

We don't shed the elements; we utilize them. Our design allows you to connect deeper with the environment. We create windows to let you experience the vistas, and decks to share stories with others. Atlas doesn't suck water and power from city pipes, it collects and recycles, like nature itself. Atlas acknowledges that individuals are not independent of the whole, but a piece of the puzzle that helps increase life rather than only destroy.

SPECIFICATIONS:

Length:	18'
Width:	8'
Height:	13' 6"
First Floor Area:	144 S.F.
Second Floor Area:	52 S.F.
Total:	196 S.F.
Rainwater collection area:	144 S.F.
Solar panel power production:	800 Watts
Composting Toilet:	Available

Unit Weight:	11,000 lbs.
Hitch Weight:	1,100 lbs.
Fresh water tank:	74 gals.
Black water tank:	47 gals.
Grey water tank:	37 gals.
Deep Cycle batteries:	4

AMENITIES:

Water heater

Backup generator

Induction cooktops

Refrigerator

Exterior electrical and sewer hookups

Interior heater

Spray foam insulation

Atlas is a new breed of RV/Tiny House, and repersents a new way of design thinking. **Aesthetics no longer solely rule the playground. Design that does, design that acts and contributes is king**. Its design is about function as much as it is about aesthetic, and it prioritizes contribution as much as communion. It minimizes dependence on the grid by collecting rainwater, using solar power, and passive cooling and heating space. It is a house that transforms from a sleek concealed traveling trailer to an open, inviting space that embraces nature both inside and out. This design is one I would like to park next to a stream.

Photo by: McCall Burau

Photo by: McCall Burau

What if a building could grow?

How do we re-examine common problems. Can we find new solutions to age old questions? I believe we can be re-designing the process and asking better questions.

Ch. 6 | **WHAT IF A BUILDING COULD GROW**

In 2003 out of 300 students, a select number are accepted into the Architecture Program at North Dakota State after their freshman year. Pretty quickly you become aware of the school's three most coveted prizes. The first being voted best Master's Thesis; second, earning the Alpha Rho Chi Award, and third, winning the fourth year High-rise competition. This partner event is often the most talked about and highly visited exhibitions at the school.

The skyscraper competition in our year was judged by the famous firm SOM (Skidmore, Owings and Merrill), and typically came with a cash prize. The goal was to design a sustainable skyscraper. The entire class flew out to San Francisco to investigate the site, meet with the firm, and get a tour of their office. Lance and I decided it was better to use our skills and strengths to work together rather than compete against each other. The professors had everyone fill out a personality test, and we had an inkling that they were going to use the results to team up opposites. Lance and I coordinated different answers to ensure we could be a team.

The semester before Skyscraper studio Lance started researching sustainable technologies, and I started researching marketing. This way we would have an edge from the very beginning. We knew that we both had great work effort, design skills, and were computer savvy. But the competition was fierce, and a lot of people would be giving it their all.

The first day we had to come up with three designs. From there Lance and I ran with it. We had 2-feet by 4-feet sheets of paper and filled up the professor's office hallway with varying designs.

One of our first designs consisted of three towers that rotated around each other. We thought this would allow more light into the building. Our professor at the time, Professor Booker, took one look and brought up a good point: the three towers were shading each other, thus negating our most important point. We needed a better story, a new guide, and a framework to make design decisions. We could spin our wheels shooting out as many different designs as we could, but they would be a waste of time if we had nothing to weigh them against. In other words, it was time to start over.

We decided that we needed to design not just the skyscraper itself, but we also spend time and effort designing our anvil, a hard concept which we could form our ideas. We needed a set of principles to steer our design, one where weak ideas would fall to the floor and where good ideas could stand the test of time on. To win this competition, the concept had to speak to sustainability, a prerequisite of the project. It also had to be memorable and plant a seed in the minds of the judges. We knew that design wasn't all that mattered, but how we conveyed and sold that design was what would win us the competition.

Our idea was: "What if a building could grow?" What would it look like, what could it do? This concept hit home. No longer was sustainability about pasting solar panels on generic looking rectangles. The question itself pushed us to solve a harder problem, to look deeper, to think harder. When most people design, they tend to think about the end result. What will the building or the product look like? Most people don't reflect on the mold that creates the final object. Fewer people are aware that they need to pour great effort into designing the process they use to make the design. Like sharpening the saw before cutting down a tree, we need to put as much thought into the design of the process as we do into the outcome. Our final product was the result of such a process.

What people don't know is that buildings are responsible for more than half of all energy consumption and global greenhouse gas emissions annually. Buildings consume significant amounts of water and energy, and they often produce none. So what could buildings do that they currently are not?

· Buildings should create energy.
· Buildings should clean the air.
· Buildings should make people healthy rather than sick.
· Buildings should revitalize our downtown urban cores.
· Buildings should feed us.

Imagine if a building could grow. What if it could produce its own water, its own food, and its own energy? What would it look like? The first thing we needed to do was investigate the soil we were going to plant our

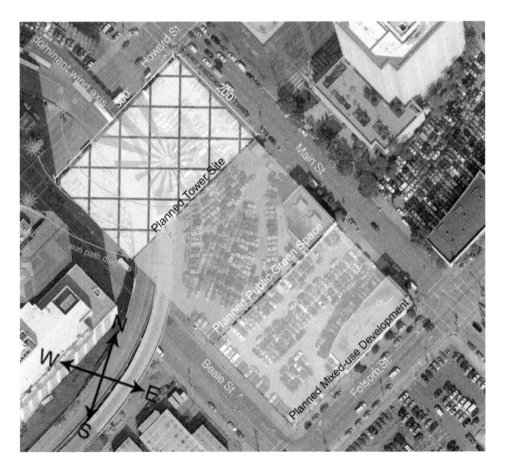

building in.

We found that our San Francisco site, currently a parking lot, had prevailing winds coming in from the northwest. These winds also brought in the fog. The southern side of the site was blanketed in sunlight.

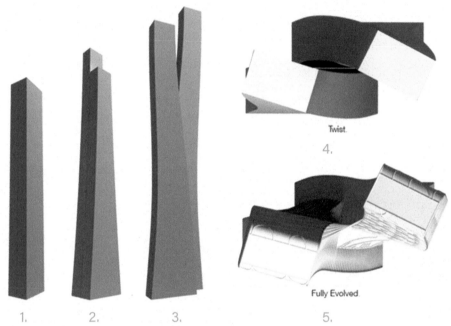

Twist.

4.

Fully Evolved.

1.   2.   3.   5.

Grow Graphic by Alex Gore and Lance Cayko

1. The natural form of a skyscraper is tall and slender.
2. First, we can taper the building to have a wider and stronger base and a narrower top for stability.
3. Then we split apart the building to let in more natural light and to create more surface area to collect solar power.
4. We then twist the tower at the top to collect the wind and fog in San Francisco. This twisting allowed the westerly winds to flow through with little resistance.
5. Finally bending the towers slightly away from each other lets the fog pass through the center for water collection. It also allows for the wind turbines located at the top of the building to capture power.

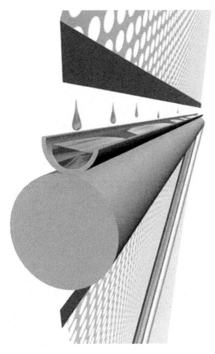

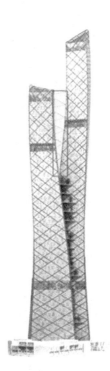

Fog Collection Graphic by Alex Gore and Lance

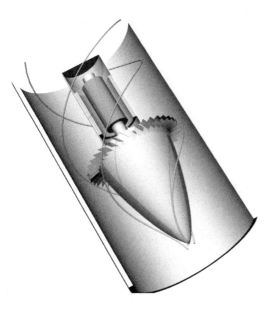

Each turbine has its own venturi tube for increased wind speed velocity, and employs a direct drive electricity generator system. The direct drive generators are also able to operate at lower rotational speeds and eliminates the normally heavy and expensive gear box.

Wind Turbine Graphic by Alex Gore and Lance

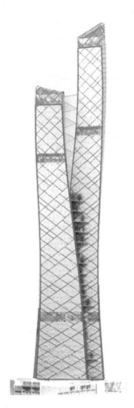

Garden Skin Graphic by Alex Gore and Lance Cayko

The fog collection system located between the buildings allows the skyscraper to capture water. It trickles down through the skin of the building to cool the building and to grow its own plants. Which in turn produce oxygen, cleans the air, and creates food for the inhabitants.

Solar panels speckle the southern side of the building in a leaf-like pattern in order not to block views and give a natural feel to the facade. These panels are perforated to let light pass through creating a relaxing shade pattern on the interior.

The double skin glass wall allows for space to grow plants, and also acts as insulation. The air trapped in-between the glass has a resistance value that helps keep the building warmer during cooler temperatures. Air is also drawn in through the buildings' skin. It passes through the plants to purify the dirty air coming in and clean the air going out. The building thus

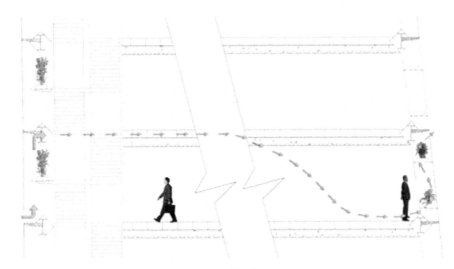

Filter Graphic by Alex Gore and Lance Cayko

acts as a giant air filter for the city.

Office space, even in the winter months, generally requires cooling because of the high concentration of people and machines. By placing the office levels below the residential levels, we can pull warm air through the

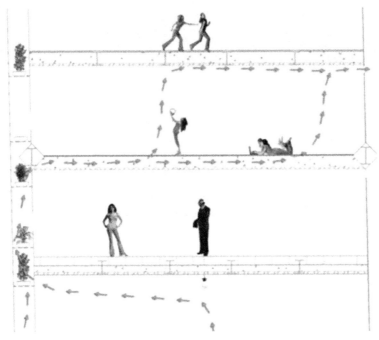

Filter Graphic by Alex Gore and Lance Cayko

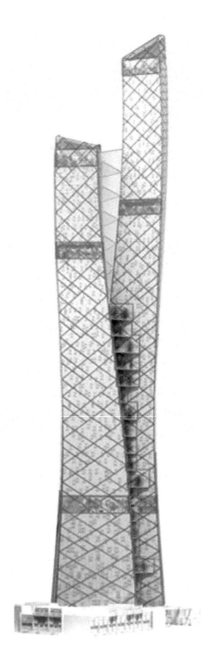

Green Space Graphic by Alex Gore and Lance Cayko

window skin wall, purify it, and use the heat to warm the residences above.

We included a social element as well. Public green spaces are provided throughout the building to help foster a better connection to the environment and the community residing within it.

26th Floor

25th Floor

Skip-stopGraphic by Alex Gore

In order to focus on the quality of living of the inhabitants we used a skip-stop apartment to ensure the best views for everyone. That means that the entrance of your apartment is on one level—for example, the 25th floor—and the majority of your apartment is on the 26th floor. This way your apartment can have views on both sides of the city.

In this case a backyard view of the bay with a balcony, and a front yard view of the city. It also reduces the number of floors the elevator has to stop at, thus making it more efficient. And, only every other level is serviced by a hallway.

View of the bay.Rendering by Lance Cayko

Bay side view. Rendering by Lance Cayko

City side view. Rendering by Lance Cayko

One thing you will notice is that the structure is nestled between the glass walls on the exterior of the building. The pattern of the structure is triangular yet irregular. We started with the triangular shape, the form with the most effective strength to efficiency ratio. During our tour of SOM (Skidmore, Owings & Merrill) they presented a tower in which they arranged the post and beams in an asymmetrical pattern. When they ran this design through testing, they found that it performed better than the traditional layout. They told us this is because when the building moved the asymmetrical pattern allowed forces to move into other areas of the structure to spread out the load. In a uniform structural pattern, there are no areas where extra forces can be compensated. It's a great idea, so we mimicked it in our building

The San Francisco skyscraper sits on the opposite side of downtown from the Trans American world tower—an iconic part of the city's skyline. The shape of our skyscraper is complimentary to that of the Trans American, and together they seem to bookend the City by the Bay.

Our efforts led Lance and me to win the coveted Skyscraper prize.

Location Graphic by Alex Gore

After this, there were only two more prizes everyone wanted. We ended up splitting them, with Lance winning the coveted Peter F. McKenzie Memorial Endowment Award for best thesis. I won the Alpha Rho Chi Medal, bestowed by the faculty to the one student who best exemplifies leadership, service, and the promise of professional merit.

Life's best solutions come from asking better questions. Steve Jobs didn't just ask how to make a portable music player. Sony could do that. He asked what was the most beautiful and straightforward way to get music to your ears.

Marcus Aurelius, who you might know as the Caesar in the movie Gladiator, was also the Caesar that wrote the book Meditations. One of his points was to "Look beneath the surface: never let a thing's intrinsic quality or worth escape you" (12). I take this as an imperative to ask deep questions. Start by asking what you are designing and what it wants to do. What is its true purpose? Don't take the easy answer. Don't be satisfied with small, simple, quick answers. Ask questions that help you grow and solve bigger problems. Examine the question you are asking. Follow the question to its logical conclusion and ask: then what? What would that do? What did that accomplish? Spend time designing the anvil, and a system to filter your solutions. What amazing solutions could you come to by asking better questions?

PART 3
LIVE

Your life is dictated by the quality of the decision you make. How you improve those decisions are a function of the feedback loop you create. A feedback loop is a structure defined by three stages: input, evaluation, adjustment.

The input stage in the creative field is the investigation / examples you find, and also the creation you make. This phase forces you to create something: an image, a prototype, a CAD model, etc...

The evaluation stage is how you judge and score the decisions you have made. Part three of this book contains the guides and checklists you need to evaluate what you have created.

7

The Checklist

Ch. 7 | **THE CHECKLIST**

Design is about creating something beautiful in a messy world. While there are principles, there is no sure-fire solution or single equation that you can use every time to get the desired result. You don't need to use every rational or creative principle in each project. Most likely you will focus on three or so concepts to help shape your design. But you must learn all of them to know which principles apply to which situation. The key is to design your process with the principles you need for your specific task.

A checklist is a tool to help you focus. This helps boil down the project to relevant tasks. Checklists have been successfully used in surgery to cut down errors, and in business to boost productivity. In his book, *The Checklist Manifesto*, Atul Gawande dissects how errors of ignorance and ineptitude can be reduced with a checklist. His main point being that no matter how much of an expert you may be, a well-designed list can improve outcomes. Studies have backed up this claim.

The checklist in this chapter has been brewed over the years and around the country, stoked in the fire of New York City, Fargo, North Dakota, and the University of Colorado, Boulder. Its ingredients were plucked from history's greatest designers. And the final recipe has been tasted by hundreds of students. The results of which have been remarkable.

Use the checklist for your next ten projects or until the process becomes so familiar to you that it becomes second nature. Write your project titles down in the list below until it is complete. Visit: **alexandergore.com/bookresources** for a print out of this list.

PROJECTS

Number	Project Name
1	_____
2	_____
3	_____
4	_____
5	_____
6	_____
7	_____
8	_____
9	_____
10	_____

To properly use creative thinking you are going to need some rules, a map, and a little gas. The rules are the design principles. The map is the design process. The gas is the intangible drive you bring to the project. It is what the army calls a force multiplier.

Different architects have used different thought processes, tools, and desires to fuel their internal drive. In Chapter Three we learned Zaha Hadid starts most designs by painting, and Steven Holl by water coloring. We learned in architecture history that Buckminster Fuller used the concept of "Spaceship Earth" as inspiration to guide his thinking.

You may not know your internal drive. You might not be able to define the spark, the fuel that lives within you. But there will be times in your life that you will glimpse the flame that burns within your soul. When you do tend to it, provide it with kindling and oxygen. Give the time and the tools it requires to develop and grow. Nurture that feeling with emotion and energy. Then you will have the gas to go farther, and be greater than you were before.

The checklist is a culmination of the previous chapters in this book. It is the combination of the three chapters in **Part One**, combined with the insight you gained from the examples in **Part Two,** and it will create a deeper understanding of the creative process.

THE CREATIVITY **CHECKLIST**

INVESTIGATE:

☐ Write your three examples.

_____   _____   _____

☐ What ideas did you take from your examples?

_____   _____   _____

☐ What's is the deep question you are trying to solve?

_____

Is this an analogy, or a first principles problem? **Ask** great questions. **What** are your opportunities? **Let** the environment be your guide. **What** is the unifying idea?

REDUCE:

Draw a line connecting three principles that will be your guide.

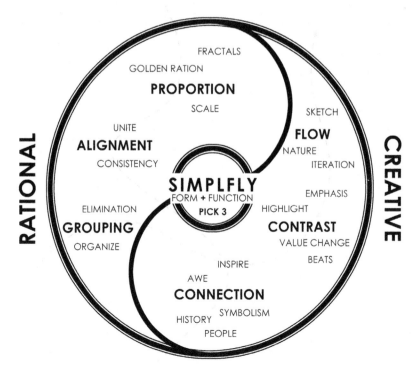

ITERATE.:

To iterate is to practice. Practice improves skill, which leads to
perfection.

☐ Dedicate the time necessary to produce iterative designs.

☐ Gather the correct tools to complete the task.

☐ Match your process with your desired outcome.

☐ Use the best ingredients (materials, tools, programs, teachers) you
can find.

☐ Explore the problem from multiple angles. Think beneath the
surface of the problem.

☐ Developed a new skill throughout the process?

EVALUATE

☐ Finalize your unifying concept or parti. Write it here:

_____

☐ Create a mockup of your presentation

☐ Use the Checkup to check in on your progress. (In the next chapter)

☐ Do your elements reinforce your concept?

Harmony is how everything comes together in your project. If even one
aspect is out of sync with the others, you will ruin your harmony. It would
be like a whole choir singing with one person out of key.

Your goal, and the creativity code, is to transform your intangible ideas
into something physical (this includes digital manifestations).

The "code" can refer to the process of encrypting symbols with secret
meaning, as in wartime, or the symbolic arrangement of instructions in a
computer program. Both are analogous to the creative design process,
where you infuse the building, poster, music, or presentation you are
creating with ideas, emotions, and meaning. When people see or listen to
what you created and connect to it, they have cracked the creativity code.

Computers can make programs, software, and games through code. They do this by manipulating numbers, words, and symbols to create their desired results. The most basic computer code is 1's and 0's. But each program, (Java, C++) has its own language and structure.

In design, you similarly enter a thought into a structure. The design process is: Investigate, Reduce, Iterate, Evaluate. From there you start to build your idea by using the design principles. GAP: Grouping, Alignment, Proportion. And FCC: Flow, Connection, Contrast, wiyh its secondary items such as scale, awe, emphasis, etc. The process and the principles create a language for you to transform thoughts into reality.

G,A,P,F,C,C,S,A,E,F,Gr,S, etc

EXAMPLE: USING THE CHECKLIST

While working at Studio Daniel Libeskind, one of the things I learned was to do what you love. Every year at our firm, we try to do at least one fun project. In 2012 there was a lot of buzz about the end of the Mayan calendar and the end of the world. Also, it seemed that hurricanes, fires, tsunamis and even tornados were becoming more prevalent. We decided to design homes that would endure the end of the world and the more turbulent weather.

CHECKLIST:

Write your three examples.

We let natural disasters be our guide. Each home would guard against either: fire, flood, earthquake or tornado. The house that guards against tornados also defends against a nuclear attack, as both come from the sky.

What ideas did you take from your examples?

The problems above are elemental problems, meaning they derive from the four basic elements: fire, water, earth, and air. As a "fun" exercise for our firm, we selected a symbol to represent each element to reduce the amount of time we spent on design. A circle, triangle, rectangle, and square would represent each type of elemental design. If we were worth our salt as designers, this limitation wouldn't hinder our creativity.

We reduced the houses to elemental shapes: Fire = Square, Flood = Rectangle, Earthquake = Triangle, Tornado = Circle

What is the deep question you are trying to solve?

Can buildings help protect us against disasters?

Is this an analogy, or first principles problem?

First Principles.

What are your opportunities?

Design some great houses, while also getting some press for the firm.

SIMPLIFY PICK THREE:

Grouping: By grouping the homes into shapes, we eliminate many designs options that could waste time.
Connection: Connecting a popular subject of the time—natural disasters—with home design.
Contrast: To highlight the difference between our designs and the

surrounding disasters all houses were designed as modern homes. This style emphasizes simple, clean lines and uncluttered designs. The design sets the homes apart from the natural environment, making them "pop" in their surroundings.

Sometimes your use of the principles will be subconscious or vague from the start. Through iteration, try and test different principles.

Have you developed a new skill throughout the process?

Yes, the tornado/nuclear house can go underground. I learned how to make an animation in 3DS Max in order to show this feature. Below are the results of the process.

EARTH |

All image in 2012 series by F9 Productions Inc.

The earth house protects against earthquakes with its shock resistant footing system, and protective skin that covers the windows.

★ ★ ★
STILL
STANDING

2012
6 PM

@DOOMSDAYDWELLINGS.COM

EARTHQUAKE SURVIVAL
SAFE DESIGN

① As an Earthquake begins to liquefy the ground turning what once was study soil into quicksand, connected flexible footings and special moment resisting frames help the building move with the ground eliminating the risk that the building will tear itself apart.

② The steel shell covers the window glazing area and acts as a protective shield and connection frame for the structure.

③ A backup generator provides essential heat and power goes out.

④ Stored food mitigates the risk of traveling on broken and battered roads to potentially unsecure stores.

⑤ A stockpile of building supplies will allow you to rebuild and help the neighborhood recover providing a necessary moral boost and gives hope to the new future.

A.

③⑤

A survival tunnel leads to an escape hatch, storage space and a power generater located in the garage.

SOCIAL (EVERYDAY) SURVIVAL
GOOD DESIGN

A. Parties can flow from the open dining/living room onto the outdoor living deck though a glass wall that opens completely to the outside.

B. An unprecedented glass canopy rhytmnically cuts though the walls and roof illuminating the vaulted interior living space.

C. A central crow's nest, echoing the idea of a child's tree fort, contains the master bed, bath and closet.

D. A separate, safe downstairs play area allows children freedom from parents - and vise versa.

The steel cover ② glides on a base track and connect to the rear of the house covering the windows. The track is at a slight tilt so that gravity can help close the structure incase of a total power failure.

Solar panels can be mounted to the south side of the upper cover.

①

Base isolation bearings minimizes the affect of the earth's movement on the home.

(see detail below)

AIR | The air house protects against tornados by being made without hard edges. The wind swirls around the home with nothing to snag on. It can also lower itself underground to guard against a nuclear attack.

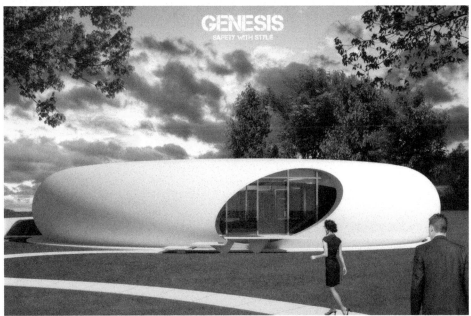

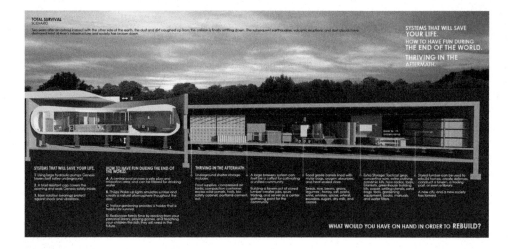

FIRE |

The Fire house shields itself from flames with its metal siding and collapsible form.

YOU HAVE A
SEED
WITH A SHELL

© DOOMSDAY
DWELLINGS.COM

FIRE SURVIVAL
SAFE DESIGN

Exterior 3,000 gallon on site water supply.   75 Ft. Defensible Space   Building closes to create a 6 Hr. fire wall.   Double vent protects air intake.

Fire Wall - Six Hour Resistance Rating

1 4 hour fire resistant metal panel
2 Reinforced concrete shell (unspecified thks)
3 4 inch fire resistant insulation. Able to withstand the intense heat of flames approaching 2150°F
4 2 layers of fire resistant plaster board.

Defensible space - 75 feet

1 Remove any flammable vegetation within 15 feet of a home's walls.
2 Mow grasses and weeds to 6 inches or less within 30 feet of structures.
3 Remove what's known as ladder fuels — shrubs and small trees — from beneath taller trees

Double fire resistant vent

1 The interior vent swells when exposed to high temperatures and up closes off the cells, effectively blocking off fire & ember intrusion.
2 Exterior low profile vent creates a maze that flying embers find hard to navigate.

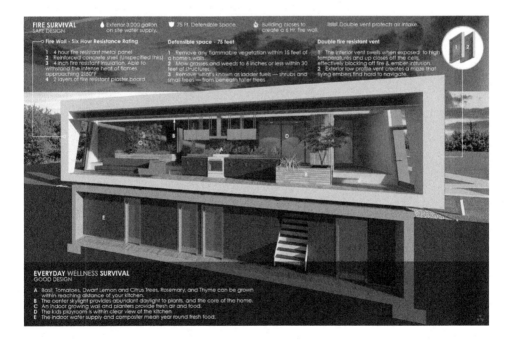

EVERYDAY WELLNESS SURVIVAL
GOOD DESIGN

A Basil, Tomatoes, Dwarf Lemon and Citrus Trees, Rosemary, and Thyme can be grown within reaching distance of your kitchen.
B The center skylight provides abundant daylight to plants, and the core of the home.
C An indoor growing wall end planters provide fresh air and food.
D The kids playroom is within clear view of the kitchen
E The indoor water supply and composter mean year round fresh food.

WATER |

The raised home design elevates the main level away from rising waters. Operable steel panels not only mitigate the problem of unwanted direct gain and glare from the east and west sun. It also alleviates the chance for debris in high water from penetrating into the residence.

The Creativity Checkup

8

Ch. 8| **THE CREATIVITY CHECKUP**

Critiques are a staple of the design process. Throughout your design process, you will or should have many checkpoints. These can be internal checks with yourself or your team. Or they can be external checkpoints with your clients, customers or other entities. Each checkpoint is a presentation.

The first thing you need to do is plan your presentation. You need to explore both the macro and the micro level of a project/design. The micro level is the outlining and storyboarding your presentation. It is about putting the major components in the right place. The macro level is the broader understanding of your task over time in context. It is what you are trying to convey and how to connect that to an audience.

If we think about presentations using the Creativity Checklist, we can start to acquire a deeper understanding of what we are doing. The big question we are solving is not, "How to give a presentation"; it's, "How to communicate my idea." To understand that question you need to start learning. Some great starting points are:

Made to Stick: Why Some Ideas Survive and Others Die
By Chip and Dan Heath
The Secret Structure of Great Talks
By Nancy Duarte. On: TED.com

If your presentation is in a week, you will not be able to read a book and watch a TED talk in time. Because of that, you need to start researching marketing now. In school (especially college), and in business, your success partly rests on your ability to communicate ideas. No matter how great your idea is no one will care if you cannot communicate it clearly. Speech class teaches the basics. It is not enough.

On the micro scale, you need to plan your presentation. That means creating a full-scale mockup. If you don't have all your images created, sketch the images and concepts you need to present.

 Doing these steps allows your audience to understand your concept fully. Doing anything less is cheating yourself. If you are not providing the full picture, completing the thought and engaging your audience than you cannot gain the feedback you need to either keep going or change tactics. To elicit dialogue, your first presentation or your "midterm" must be presented in un-finalized fashion. Meaning, do not present your initial ideas with polished renderings. If you do so, you might be wasting your time, and you won't get good feedback. The feedback will focus on final touches, colors and so forth. People won't feel comfortable examining the initial idea, which should be the focus of the first presentation.

If you are creating a PowerPoint, sketch out each slide you will use. Remember one idea per slide, and one image per idea. For larger presentations, say 24" x 36" boards, use three ideas per board. Remembering each idea should reinforce the central theme.

THE KEY IS CONSISTENCY

Designers often use themes to guide their work. In the design world, this is known as the "Parti." Meaning the central idea or theme you will carry throughout the project. The idea is that this theme connects the multiple pieces of the projects from exterior to interior, small to large together in order to create a cohesive whole. A project theme could be to mimic nature, create efficiency, or build from an inspirational idea. Designs tend to fall off when they fail to follow through with their concept.

If your theme is to blend your building into the landscape, you can accomplish this by using local materials that match that landscape, set the building lower into the ground, and follow the topography changes. If your theme centers on sustainable design, each feature could be a component of that concept. The roof could collect rainwater, the building and materials could be placed to take advantage of the sun's heat and energy, and waste could be recycled.

The goal is to be consistent. Often the major criticism of students' work is that they were not consistent with the theme they set up. Most students walk themselves into their critique. For example, one might say they selected a building site because of the great views, but would fail to orient their house or windows to take advantage of those views. Inconsistency is a dead giveaway of poor design.

In contrast, you can have two wildly different successful bridge designs. A bridge could cross counties by spanning a river. The scale could be enormous and powerful. Another bridge could span counties while only being a fraction of the size. It could be refined, sleek and elegant in its details. Both are successful because they are true to themselves.

> **PROTIP:** Write down your unifying idea and check back in on it regularly to make sure you are consistent.

The caveat to this idea came from my previous boss Carla Swickerath while working at Studio Daniel Libeskind. She told me never to let the rules take over your design. They are rules made by you, and can be broken by you.

What can happen is sometimes the initial constraints or inspiring parti might be too confining and be limiting your design. Feel free to break them knowing a new theme will come in its place that will be more appropriate.

Also, make sure to use contrast to highlight your idea. If you have the time, watch "The Secret Structure of Great Talks" by Nancy Duarte. She explains how great speeches follow a pattern. The structure of a talk, story, or presentation flows from explaining what is, to imagining what could be. Your presentation starts with either laying out the context, the background of the issue, or the inciting incident. The inciting incident is the turning point that initiates action (13). It's the gap between what is and your unifying idea. Solving that gap is what you are explaining in your presentation. This gap creates tension until the distance between the reality and your solution can be eliminated.

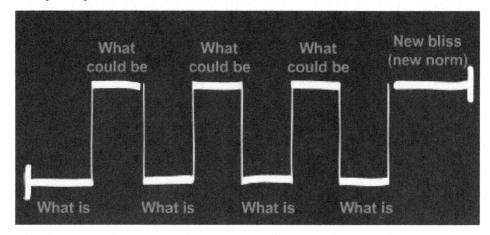

Duarte, N. (2011). The secret structure of great talks [Digital image]. Retrieved May 24, 2016, from https://www.ted.com/talks/nancy_duarte_the_secret_structure_of_great_talks

CHECKLIST INTRODUCTION

Use the checkup below before starting your presentation. It serves to help you determine whether you are on the right track, just as you would go to your doctor to get a checkup to sure you're healthy.

Over the hundreds of design presentations I have seen, the biggest problem is aligning intent with action. Alignment isn't only for organizing physical space; it can be used to organize thoughts and ideas. Use the checklist below to reassess your plans, either before a presentation or as an internal audit.

THE **CREATIVITY CHECKUP**

What deep question are you solving?

_____

What is unifying concept or parti? Write it here:

_____

Mockup:
- ☐ Outline your presentation to scale.
- ☐ Is every idea represented by an image?

Review:
- ☐ Eliminate any unimportant task that cannot be completed in time.
- ☐ Do your elements reinforce your concept?
- ☐ Does your design match the intent of your idea? How?

  _____

- ☐ Do your images match the emotion of your project? How?

  _____

- ☐ What do you need to change so that your initial ideas match your manifestation?
- ☐ What unique aspect will you bring your audience?

  _____

Practice:
- ☐ Practice your presentation three times. Have friends watch you if they are willing. Practice at the place you will be presenting if possible.
- ☐ Was your presentation complete and was it clear? Record yourself if necessary and listen to the playback. Most smartphones can do this.

Have a backup:
  Did you email your file to the host ☐, yourself☐, and did you bring a copy on a USB?☐

EXAMPLE:

In third year studio, we had a design competition and were asked to design an addition to a concrete factory. It seemed mundane enough. What could you do with a concrete factory? What questions could you ask that could help influence its design? The program was to create a new lobby, more office space, and expand the factory floor. This competition was sponsored by the concrete factory and came with a winning prize of $300 – $500 (I can no longer recall the exact figure).

Creating a "green" concrete factory didn't appear to hit the mark. Applying different aesthetics for aesthetic's sake never seems to be an option for me. So where to begin?

Long before this studio I realized others had talents beyond my own. I needed an edge, something that would help me out. I needed knowledge, inspiration, and information others did not have. I wanted to create a bigger net in order to catch more ideas, and build on the shoulders of giants. Most students looked at architecture magazines, and some roamed the architecture aisles perusing through books—which I also did. But I wanted to go further and dive deeper, so my grandma gave me her old school TiVo, which was, in fact, a VCR. In the library, I discovered a vast collection of videos and dove into them. One particular video explained that placing objects that periodically interrupt the view, you could highlight the contrast between the foreground and the background, making people perceive this difference.

This idea of forcing perception of space took hold of me. When someone, maybe a potential client comes to the factory, what would the owner want them to look at and why? What would the owners want the building to say about them? How could architecture speak to them?

The most logical place to start in not the entrance to the building, but the entrance to the site itself. What different questions can we ask? Can a building help build a brand? Can it help sell, explain, and tell a story of what a company does?

During the presentation of the design, I had in front of my feet four concrete blocks laid down horizontally end to end touching each other in the typical fashion you would build a CMU (concrete masonry unit) wall.

Photo by: Alex Gore

I started to explain that as you enter the site, the driveway would wrap you past the new addition. Typically, concrete precast walls are joined together like you see before me. End to end tight together. But if you construct your walls slightly different you would drive past the new addition you would see slivers of light cutting through the walls every twenty feet along its whole height.

As I was explaining this, I slowing pulling each concrete brick up vertical. The brittle edges of the concrete broke off into tiny pieces as it scratched against the tile floor. The crackling of the concrete caught the audience's attention. I stood them up with a 4-inch gap between each other. These CMU blocks represent the 20' tall precast concrete, which the factory makes, and by separating them with glass, you can highlight them through the contrast of mass and void. As a car passes by the blocks would be silhouetted at night as the light passes through them creating a rhythm of uniqueness that produces a memory.

Photo by: Alex Gore

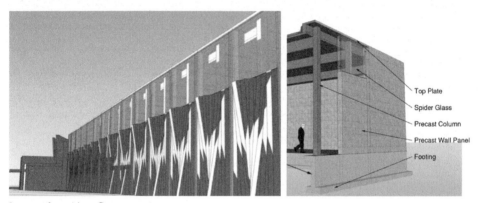

Image by: Alex Gore

The entrance of the concrete factory wanted to reveal something new out of something familiar. It was a transition from the outside of the building to inside which gave me a hint about what materials to use. The outer shape resembled the form of the concrete truck that runs up and down the streets of all of our hometowns. The inside roof was made of glass and below it hung a rebar (which stands for reinforcement bar), which is normally placed inside of concrete to make it stronger. By exposing a material that is normally on the inside of concrete, you flip the perspective of the visitor giving them a unique 'insider' feel. The entrance is the transition point from the outside world into the world of concrete.

By exposing the rebar, we give the public a view of something unique

Image by: Alex Gore

to that industry. Hanging down from this rebar are lights pointed towards the outer wall, and against these outer walls hang large examples of concrete pieces that showed the different texture and stains that that company could apply. This idea came from the nature of the problem itself and asking questions. How can I utilize what I am building to solve multiple problems at once? What value can I add to the client besides just building the physical space?

RECAP

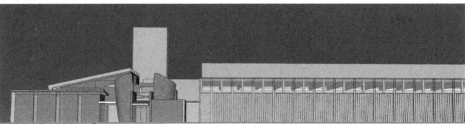

Image by: Alex Gore

Use the checkup to check-in on the health of your project at least a week before your midpoint review and final presentation.

THE **CREATIVITY CHECKUP**

What deep question are you solving? What is unifying concept or parti? Write it here: <u>Can a building help sell a product?</u>

Mockup:
- ☑ Outline your presentation to scale.
- ☑ Is every idea represented by an image?

Review:
- ☑ Eliminate any unimportant task that cannot be completed in time.
- ☑ Do your elements reinforce your concept?
- ☑ Does your design match the intent of your idea?
  <u>Yes, the walls, windows, and spaces reinforce the properties and benefits of concrete.</u>
- ☑ Do your images match the emotion of your project?
  <u>Yes, the nighttime image was not common at that point in schooling. I thought it was necessary to reinforce my design intent.</u>
- ☑ What do you need to change so that your initial ideas match your manifestation?
- ☑ What unique aspect will you bring your audience?
  <u>Lugging in 28 lbs. concrete units and moving them during the presentation to highlight a point.</u>

NEXT STEPS

Remember, even if you do not need to give a presentation or a "midpoint" you can use this **Checkup** to take stock of where you are. It can be your internal audit to see how you are doing. The key is the effort you put into the review. You need to examine your project and determine whether you are meeting your goals.

Depending on your results you will either need to rethink your project, or push ahead to completion. If there are major issues, go through the checklist in the previous chapter to rethink your design. If you only have minor adjustments, you can move forward.

After completing this exercise, redesign and reevaluate as necessary. Then list out the remaining drawings, views, or renderings you need to complete your project and attack them systematically. When completing your final design always push yourself to learn something new. With each new rendering I complete, I typically look up a new rendering or Photoshop technique to learn. This way you grow yourself while doing the work you have to do anyway, and stay current in your field alowing you to lead from the front.

The Secret

Find the universal truth to design, and the secret to trasformation by looking within. The process of success starts by digging into who you are.

Ch. 9 | **THE SECRET**

Physical places are simply mirages, reflections of an inner world, the world of your thoughts. So to get from "here" to "there," you must do your manipulating within.

- Mike Dooley

The last assignment in the engineering course Lance and I teach is to design a bridge or a house. Lance and I spend this third of the semester individually stopping by each student's desk to help them solve the unique problems they might be having. Through these interactions, we get to know the students, their personalities, their quirks and their nuances.

Two weeks before the final project is due we teach them how to render and make their project really stand out. We then fade in the distance, stop visiting them and let them put their final presentation together. Lance and I have a good idea of what the students are designing, but the end result is always a transformation from what we saw a couple of weeks before. Designs go from black and white to full color rendered environments with a story and theme.

Most of the projects are well thought out and are nicely presented. The most fascinating aspect of this whole process is the ability of these designs to mirror the intangible essence of the student who created them. Manifested in a 3D building or bridge is the inner soul of the students. Not only are the obvious forces like effort, determination or a lack of caring shown but the nuance of their personality is exposed. Elegance, refinement, sloppiness, drive, storytelling, professionalism, or bullshit are all exposed for everyone to see. Who they are has escaped their body and now lives in a separate form in the world as their design.

One student designed a home in the shape of a black diamond whose true beauty and wonder could only be revealed by peering inside. It was a reflection of her personality. She was shy, closed off, someone who you might not approach for a conversation. But when you did you found out how warm, deep and engaging she was.

Another student was elegant and a gifted speaker. She was soft spoken but deliberate with her word choices. Her vocabulary consisted of nuanced word choices that cut directly to the point. Her house was the a mirro of who she was: subtle yet powerful, deliberate and refined.

Another student was charismatically gifted. He was charming and very nice. He had the ability to bring people together and could connect with you in conversation. His design was a bridge that connected two counties together in order to increase trade and the economies of both regions. I could not be more proud of these students. From freshmen to seniors, they are producing professional level work.

Over the course of the project, it became evident to the students that their internal process produces their external result. Your designs are a reflection of you. And the secret is that there are no secrets. Eventually, people are going to see through the facade you have created and know your true self. Too often we spend time creating a false image of ourselves. We present to the world a glossy image of who we are and what we do. We hide the mess that made us.

It is time to stop trying to hide or pretend to be something different. Stop spending time covering up who you are, and spend it building up your foundations from fundmentals. A new paint job on a house with a crumbling foundation is still going to fall. Your friends and family members know the real you, and that's who really matters. Now just make the "you" they know into something better. There is a world within you as rich, diverse, and interesting as the world around you. Search in there for truth and understanding. Refine your soul to find beauty. Then when you create something, it will be authentic. That authenticity leads to truth; truth leads to trust, and trust is how the world gets things done. Your design come from within, so the secret to design, is to design yourself.

> As below, so above; and as above so below.
> With this knowledge alone you may work miracles.
>
> **From Fulcanelli**
> (The Emerald Tablet of Hermes translated from French by Sieveking)

CREATIVITY IN CONTEXT

I have read many books over the years that often have amazing information that is useful and practical. I hope this book is one of those for you. While I hope you apply the lessons in this book, but I want to leave you with something different.

Each year around New Years, I come up with a resolution like many people do. Normally this is only a word or phrase that conveys an idea I want to carry through the year. For example: "Connection," "Experiment," "Discipline," etc. In 2016 a concept came to mind in a dream that I didn't fully comprehend, but I wanted to go with anyway.

Imagine for a second that everything you knew or loved was taken from you. Your family never existed. Your accomplishments didn't matter, and your experiences never occurred. This life, your real life, was just a dream. You really lived on another planet made entirely of concrete. People went to sleep to live in dreams like the movie *The Matrix*.

I woke up from this dream, in shock of that world and grateful for the one I live in now. Now I view life through a new lens as if I was plucked out of some other reality and placed in this new situation. I could see I had a wife lying by my side, and a house around me. I could hear the chickens rustling outside, and the neighbor starting his old beat up truck.

My perspective started to shift. The concept "Second Start" came to mind. The idea was that I was no longer shackled to my past choices, habits, or place in life. This was not to shirk responsibility but to allow me to be free and look through life with a new lens. I was put in this new reality completely free to start consciously making better choices.

We have two lives, and the second begins when we realize we only have one.

Confucius

In that spirit I offer to you a saying that I hope sticks with you and guides you to a more beautiful, lively second start: **Do Great Work, Learn Some Rules, and Share with Others.** The hardest aspect of advice will not be in understanding, but in implementation. The transition from empty slogans to application requires discipline. True rewards do not come from plans, but by sowing principles into the practice of your life.

DO GREAT WORK:

Life comes at a cost, no matter what you are doing time ticks away taking seconds, minutes and moments that cannot return You might think, my boss dictates my work. I have no freedom to do great work. If that's the case, then you must do the shitty work well. You must do the job you are directed to do at such a high level that when you do have a suggestion on how to do something better your boss will take note.

If you are pounding nails place them precisely and efficiently. If you are digging ditches, dig the most perfect ditch imaginable. If you're in a dead-end job, find the time to do what you love outside of work. It might take some trial and error, or iterations if you want to use design language.

For example, I tried working out every Monday, Wednesday, and Friday at 5:00 am. After four months I quit. My answer wasn't to stop working on myself it was to be more consistent. I moved workouts to after work and then woke up at 5:30 am every morning to write this book.

The key is to take responsibility for what you are doing and demand a high standard. The best students out of the hundreds we have taught, had one thing in common. It wasn't age, skin color, ethnicity, gender, religion or intelligence level. It was creating a high standard and putting in the effort to reach that standard. That's it. If you point yourself to the right goal, which can be hard, 80% of success is having a high standard and putting in the effort. 10% is luck, 10% is connections. If you don't have luck and connections, you will still be more successful than most of the people around you.

The reason this is so important is that being the best gets you disproportionate results. For example, when Michael Jordan was at his height in 1997 he scored 881 points. Karl Malone finished second with 780 points, or 88.5% of Jordan (14). Karl Malone's salary that year was $5.1 million (15). What do you think Michael Jordan's salary was? $5.6 million, $6 million, $7 million, maybe double or triple? In fact, Michael Jordan's 1997 salary was $33.1 million (16). Over six times the next leading scorer.

Most people want to move up in the ladder, do great things, be important, and make an impact on the world. Your eye is often looking towards the future. But the best way to move towards your future goal is to do what you are doing now well. Build a great foundation.

LEARN SOME RULES:

Life is a game with many different levels. High school, college, career— these are some of the many levels that can be played. Your family, friends, spouse and kids are the multiplayer modes of this game. Each level can be played better with strategy, which is simply the art and science of marshaling your resources for the most efficient and effective use (17).

To do so, you must clearly define your purpose, then test different rules to create your strategy to complete your end goal. The good thing is someone else has already done what you want to do, and they have probably written a book about it (18).

Creativity and design are two of many different tool sets you can use to play the game of life. I encourage you to use the ideas you have learned here in different areas of your life. But no one system can be an all encompassing answer. Whether it is business or baseball, learn from the best you can and apply the knowledge. Too often we read or hear some advice but don't practice it.

No one would ever think that even the best hitter in baseball could teach you the mechanics of swinging the bat so well that you would then be able to hit in the major leagues without practice. But often this is exactly what we expect when we read a book, listen to a podcast, or hear a talk. Knowing without doing is nothing. Practice, practice, practice what you learn by applying the lessons to your life.

The rules you learn should be used to inform a process. A process should be strategic, and purposeful. For example, when Jamie Foxx was creating his standup routine he would travel to a black part of the U.S., say Los Angeles, and do what he would call "white jokes." He would note which ones received laughs and cut those that did not. He would then travel to a white part of the country, like Grand Junction, Colorado, and do "black jokes." Again noting which jokes worked and which ones bombed. This way when he combined his acts, it would play well to both audiences (19).

By focusing on designing his process, he was able to achieve a better outcome. His process was strategic in creating a set that played to a wide audience. It was authentic, internally consistent world: true to itself in scope, depth, and detail (Robert Mckee "Story 186). It was also purposeful in creating an act for a comedian that successfully straddled two worlds. The hidden key behind all of this is having the discipline to follow through.

SHARE WITH OTHERS:

One of our most basic desires in life is the need for connection. It is the lifeblood of our society. This book is based on the idea that we all benefit by sharing our knowledge and insights. While teaching at the University of Colorado, we share the tools, templates, and models that make our business successful. This keeps us innovating and provides us with future employees that know our system.

You might think that sharing gives away your secrets, or hurts you in some way. But sharing is a transformative way of thinking. First sharing and teaching others will force you to understand the issues from multiple angles. It has been said that you don't truly know something until you teach it to others.

Second, the act of sharing makes you a trusted resource for others. People will see you as a leader, come to you for help, and seek your advice. You will have a greater command of the subject and eliminate doubt. A lot of frustration in life comes from insecurity which is a problem derived from a lack of confidence in what you are doing. Positioning yourself as the teacher forces you to take on new responsibilities. By understanding the information, you eliminate the concerns you had.

Find a way to teach others about: grouping, alignment, contrast or connection. Help them out on a presentation, paper, or an idea they have using the checklist.

> **SIDE NOTE:** Give/loan out your copy of this book. And I would like to personally ask for a review from wherever you purchased this book. It would not only help me out, but it would help others choose if they want to read this book.

Sharing what you learn with others is personally fulfilling, and rewarding. You might notice that this book loosely follows that mantra. **Do great work.** I have done my best to pour my heart and soul into this book and the designs it shares. The book provides some rules from which you can see life in a different light. **Learn some rules.** And by **sharing with others,** hopefully you, as well as I, have gained a deeper understanding of creativity and design.

WHAT TO DO NEXT

Everything you have learned in this book will rest on your skill: your ability to do something well. My favorite example of the power of skill is a project where professional artists recreated children's drawings. It is called *The Monster Project*. Artist take sketches that a child made and using their skills: proportions, shading, depth, color control, etc. make those ideas come to life.

http://www.Gomonsterproject.com/ Artist: gianlucamaruotti@gmail.com

Ideas are cheap; execution is expensive. Invest in yourself to develop the skills and toolset you need to participate in the creative economy. This new economy is more than artist and musicians. It is Apple, Google, Tesla and much more. It is your job, your future, the glass ceiling and the ladder. Millions of people now have access to amazing creation tools. Sketchup, a design software can be easily learned. 3D printers can create designs on demand. Websites are no longer only for business, or even bloggers. The next personal online place for expression is not Facebook, Twitter, or Instagram. It will be your own personal website. Services like Weebly and Squarespace are making it easier and easier to put up your own website, quickly, easily, beautifully and for free.

You must develop your skill with the creative tools and programs listed below. The training is broken down into three categories. A link is provided for each of the training videos. The first category is for everyone interested in developing and practicing their design muscles. The second category is for the architectural profession and the last group for businesses. Each one will increase your design and creativity skill set.

EVERYONE:

Sketching: 65% of the population is comprised of visual thinkers (20). Learning how to sketch can help connect both sides of your brain. Unlock your creativity by developing the eye-hand coordination and confidence through thinking and communicating with sketching. The appendix chapters in this book will show you easy and painless ways to start sketching out your ideas.

Visit: Alexanderkgore.com/bookresources for free training videos on the following topic:

Website: Having your own website is the Facebook of the future. Learn how to create a simple, beautiful, user-friendly websites.

Photoshop: This is an essential tool for the beginning designer. This program will teach you how to touch up your photos, create posters and other graphics you will need.

SketchUp: Start creating your ideas in the easiest, and free to use computer-aided design program.

ARCHITECTURE STUDENTS AND PROFESSIONALS:

Revit: Learn the most widely used architectural design program on the market. Learn how buildings get built and how to model to save you time. We have taught this program to 1,000's of students and professionals with raving success. The program is very encompassing. It provides tutorials on how to make Revit components, residential, and commercial projects, and miscellaneous videos on all the questions we have had over the years. It also has templates to start from and over 300 top-of-the-line components made for you.

To get started visit: Revitfurniture.com/bookdiscountdeal.com
(Not Free)

BUSINESSES:

Book bundles. Working in isolation is hard. To change a culture, you need a team on the same page.
Live Business Courses: The Creativity Culture, Design Principles and Process, Sketching, Visual notes, and Communication.

Go to the contact page and ask for special pricing on bundles of books, or courses.

Alexanderkgore.com/contact

START DESIGNING:

Pick a project to start applying what you have learned. You can go with your gut and start on something now that you know you would love to do. Or, take some time and find a strategic, authentic, and purposeful problem to solve. Then make sure you are doing great work, learning from the best, and sharing what you are doing. Throughout the process use the knowledge you have gained here with the **Checklist** and **Checkup**.

For example, you could start a blog with the knowledge you have gained in your industry or work, but share it through your lenses. The way you would have liked to be taught. Some other ideas are:

- Your own personal website
- A website for an idea you have. It could be business or personal.
- Redesign your presentations
- Reexamine a project at work, or at home.
- Help others on their journey

Pick one for now. If it is truly what you want to do than make the time for it. If you chose something and found that it is not your thing, then drop it, but only after putting in significant effort in that project. Sometimes we only quit because we are uncomfortable with what we are creating. Normally this is because our taste is more developed than our skill. Take the time to develop the skill before quitting and then decide if what you are doing is for you.

If you find something you have always wanted to do in life, make time for yourself. Get up at 5:30 am every day and work on the project you love for one hour. That way by 6:30 am you will have already accomplished something you have wanted to do before starting your normal day. No matter what you do, always be authentic.

"You don't get what you want in life; you get what you make."
Lance Cayko

APPENDIX

Sketching is a continuing source of learning
rather than a string of performances.

Paul Laseau

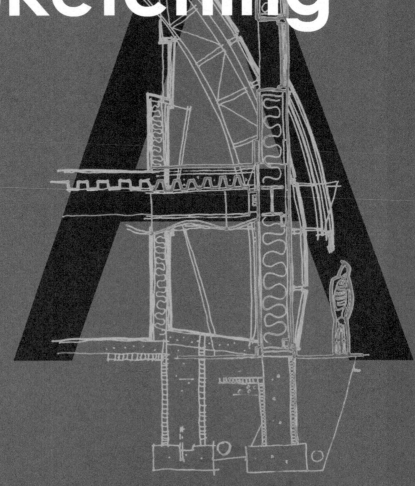

Appendix A
Sketching

APPENDIX A | **SKETCHING**

Drawing can reveal much about you to yourself, some facets of you that might be obscured by your verbal self. Your drawings can show you how to see things and how you feel about things.

Betty Edwards

The New Drawing on the Right Side of the Brain

This chapter is about reawakening the connection between the visual portion of your brain and the analytical side of your brain. You have the tools to think visually locked inside you, even if you haven't used them in a while. As the quote above suggests, drawing can reveal connections that you might not have noticed or considered before.

Sketching ideas, thoughts, products, or the existing environment pushes us to think differently, to encode in a unique way. This new way of thinking can lead to a fresh perspective on a current problems. Visual thinking can also act as a natural memory aid.

A common perception of memory is that it is a function of recall. Modern science points out that the formation of a memory is essentially encoding. In school, we are taught to learn by memorizing facts and concepts. We input facts through repetition or link them to things we already know.

You might have heard of the term "Memory Palace." It refers to a concept in which you place thoughts and ideas into a created space in your mind. This space could be your house or a building. In order to remember, mentally walk through that space to recall what you placed within it. The palace you create—and the different rooms inside it—acts as a trigger for specific memories.

The popular book *Moonwalking with Einstein* by Joshua Foer, a bestselling book on memory and one I highly recommend, opens with the story of catastrophe in fifth-century Greece. A banquet hall collapsed, trapping the bodies of those killed in the debris. Desperate family members were clawing at the wreckage in the futile attempt to recover their lost loved ones from the rubble. The few bodies that were recovered were unrecognizable and it seemed these grieving families would never have the closure they sought.

How could they piece together what happened?

"Poet Simonides of Ceos the lone survivor sealed his senses to the chaos around him and reversed time in his mind. The piles of marble returned to pillars... the splinters of wood poking above the ruins once again became a table.... He saw Scopas laughing at the head table, a fellow poet sitting across from him...

Simonides opened his eyes. He took each of the hysterical relatives by the hand and carefully stepping over the debris, guided them, one by one, to the spots on the rubble where their loved ones have been sitting.

At that moment, according to legend, the art of memory was born."
(Foer, 1)

Sketching is the internalization of the physical world. With sketching, we can better understand and remember the places and things we see. There are a few techniques that if practiced can help you confidently sketch your ideas.

For what it's worth, I am not asking you to become Da Vinci. In fact, most professional architects are mediocre sketchers. That's is because sketching isn't the end goal. For architects communication of a concept in your design/sketch is the truly desired result, not the beauty of the drawing itself. Google "Steven Holl sketches" if you doubt me. He is an amazing architect, but hardly an impressive drawer.

So let's start to prime your brain to think differently. The first step to sketching is getting comfortable drawing different types of lines. I've included a couple of techniques to ease you into putting pen to paper. If you have a sketchbook, I recommend having it with you right now and practicing each technique as we go along. If not, feel free to right in the book. Use the blank areas provided to try out the tips on your own.

THE OVERDRAW

The first technique is to rid yourself of the notion that your sketching must be precise or perfect. Let yourself be free and unattached to what is known as perfection. What I want you to do is overdraw your corners. Instead of trying to stop at a perfect point, draw slightly past the place you wish to stop. What this does is trick the mind of the viewer. It tells the viewer not to be concerned with the perfection of the drawing, but to look

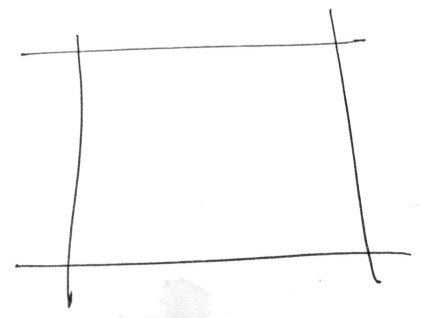

at the broader concept. This idea is so popular that the computer program Sketchup, which has 30 million users, lists overdrawn extensions as one of its styles. As a final note on the overdraw, when it comes to this technique do not be afraid to draw a strong, confident line.

WIGGLY LINE

Another common practice that follows the same logic of the overdraw technique is to give your lines a slight wiggle. Instead of drawing perfectly straight lines, allow the lines to be loose and carry a back and forth wiggle. Doing so slows down the drawing process, making the commitment to a line less consequential. Whole drawings can be completed with this technique.

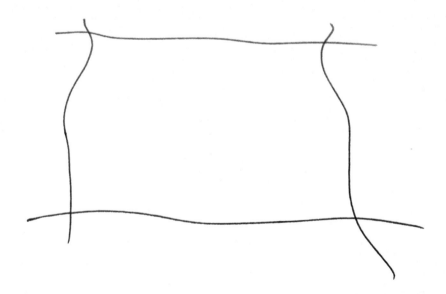

AIRPLANE

The airplane technique is one of the most fun tips to practice. Focus on the tip of your pencil as it glides down to your paper. Remember to feel yourself "pull" the pencil. Think of how an airplane glides gently to the runway. Then pull your pencil up for a smooth, gentle takeoff. What this technique accomplishes is the creation of a soft starting and ending point. Lines can blend into one another, making it easier to attach new lines to the endpoints.

When you create lines with sharp starting and ending points and attempt to add onto the line, you create a darker section or point, which can look like a mistake. Creating soft points will allow you to blend lines together.

You can see the difference between working with hard points and working with soft points where you can barely see the intersection of the lines.

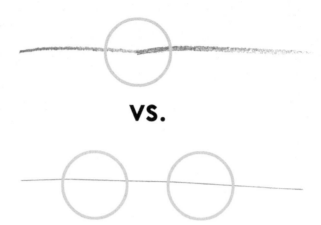

VS.

Hand Positioning

Most people start sketching or drawing without thinking about how the pencil is placed in their hands. You probably didn't consider the positioning of your pencil within your hand while drawing the techniques in the previous pages. The way you hold a pen or pencil can either hinder or improve the flexibility of your drawing skills. Try the techniques below to free your hand.

Arcs

Drawing arcs will become easier once you understand the mechanics. The size of the arch you can draw comfortably and accurately is directly related to the pivot point you have. To draw a small arc, grasp your drawing utensil close to the tip. Use only your fingers as a pivot point to draw (Image 1). "**D**" represents distance. For a medium arch, choke up on the pencil so that you have a bigger arc to pivot with (Image 2). All this is done with the wrist planted on the paper or desk. In order to make even larger curves move your pivot point back to yout wrist (Image 3). You can even move the pivot point to your elbow. I once joked while demonstrating on a backboard in a lecture that you could continue this train of thought and use your hips as your pivot point keeping everything else stiff. As I gyrated back and forth for the amusement of the class, and to my astonishment, I discovered the ease of which an arc appeared. The key thing to remember with arcs is to mind your anchor/pivot points.

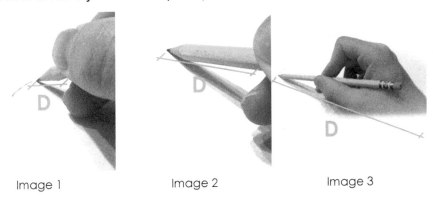

Image 1   Image 2   Image 3

Circles

The secret to circles is movement. Hold the hand with your drawing utensil two inches above the paper, and move it in a circular motion without touching the paper. Get the feel for the size and the shape of your circle before bringing your hand down onto the paper. Now lower your drawing utensil to the paper and draw the circle multiple times. With each pass your hand will start to autocorrect, essentially circling in on the circle. The concept here is the same as the overdraw. You are not trying to create a perfect circle in one pass, but allowing yourself multiple loops to convey to yourself the concept of a circle. The second way is to find an object such as a quarter, a cup, etc. to trace around.

TIP: Don't be afraid to rotate the page. Drawing feels most comfortable when your wrist is resting on a solid surface. If your hand placement can't complete an arch or whatever else you are going for then simply turn the notebook so you can easily continue the sketch.

SHADING | DEPTH

Shading gives perspective and depth to a sketch. The first rule of thumb is that objects closer in the sketch are darker and heavier, while the background is grayer and lighter. This effect can be achieved through line weight, pen/pencil pressure, re-drawing over and over a line, and shading. Some strategies you can use are listed below.

Grass

Take your pencil and push down hard on the paper, then flick your wrist up releasing the pressure. This technique can be used to create grass, shading, or an exercise allowing you to practice your eye-hand coordination. To do this, draw two independent grasses at different angles. Now connect these pieces with intermittent grasses so that they blend together.

Crosshatch

You probably remember this from drawing class. By increasing or decreasing the spacing between the crosshatch you create a darker or lighter shadow/shading area.

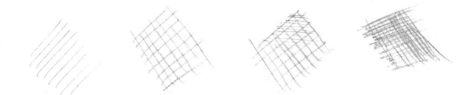

Smudge

One technique that is most effective for me is to smudge. First, lay down some graphite to work with by tilting the pencil on its side and moving back and forth. Then you can take your finger and push or pull the extra graphite around.

Perspective

The most important thing to know when creating 3D spaces or drawings is that the lines in a space follow a pattern. Commonly people are taught about the one point and two-point perspective. These are great guides to get you started.

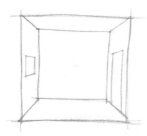

One Point Perspective   Two Point Perspective

To practice, it is helpful to sketch the space that you are in. Similar to most perspectives, the space you are occupying does not neatly sit in the center of a page. Be aware that the one or two points that are the center of focus for your drawing might be in a unique location like the image below. Try creating a rectangle of the back wall first then build your lines from there.

Relationships/Relativity

Another key concept is that once your framework is complete, it is time to find relationships. For example, the kitchen island is half the length of the railing. The Island height is same as the couch height and width. How far away does one item start from another? These relationships can be explored once you have your framework in order.

DESIGN EXERCISE |

Using a Number Two pencil, sketch a room, and detail it using the techniques above. A detail would be anything smaller than one-inch by one-inch. It could be a railing, your cat, a table setting, etc. A room could be anything bigger than a bedroom and also including an exterior scene. If you are reading this book with someone, make a plan to complete the exercise and show your results to each other.

This chapter is only a primer to get you started. The next chapter will show you how to start designing using sketching. There you will learn how to take the skills you just learned, combine them with the ideas in your head and put them down on paper. This is the first step in making your dreams come true. On the next page are some students sketches right after learning these techniques.

(sketch 2)

Sketch by Anni Huang

Sketch by Helen Purcell

Sketch by Beth Diamond

Appendix B
Constructing Design

APPENDIX B | CONSTRUCTING DESIGN

Now that we have laid a good foundation in sketching, let's put your skill to use. The visual part of your brain is incredibly powerful. In this chapter, you will learn how to sketch your ideas so you can convey your thoughts to others.

THE THUMBNAIL SKETCH

The thumbnail sketch gets its name from its size, about as big as your thumb. What makes this type of drawing effective is that it relieves the pressure to "sketch well." Its small scale makes skill a non-factor and allows you to do multiple sketches quickly. The idea is to get your emotions on paper. You are not looking for accuracy, but to unleash your intuition. By sketching small, you are freeing yourself to take a risk. Below is an example of thumbnail sketches for a cliff house by Alex Hogrefe.

Image by: Alex Hogrefe | https://visualizingarchitecture.com/

Below is an image of a cliff. Imagine you are going to build a house on this landscape. What would that house look or feel like? What form should it take?

Image: Flat Cliff in the Sea | http://miriadna.com/

In the space below, draw a quick thumbnail sketch. If you have more than one idea, sketch out two. Try using quick, confident lines.

Sketch   Floorplan

Here is a sketch made on my iPad. As you can see, it did not take longer than a minute. The first thing I did was draw the context to encode the essence of the island in my mind. My thought was to nestle the home in the vegetative area and use the sharp angles of the island to inform the shape of the floor plan.

Use thumbnail sketches as a gateway drug to thinking visual. Don't put too much pressure on yourself. Just ease into it.

BUBBLE DIAGRAM

A bubble diagram, or a mind map, is an excellent way to organize ideas. This is because it places ideas in relationship to each other through space. They add lines between ideas to convey their connection.

On the next page is an example from one of our students. On the left is a bubble diagram of how he wanted the spaces laid out. Each circle is labeled, and he even color-coded the diagram so he could align the spaces above on the second floor with the sizes of the rooms on the main floor. His main idea was for each room to have two views. You can see on the right how his idea came to fruition later in the semester.

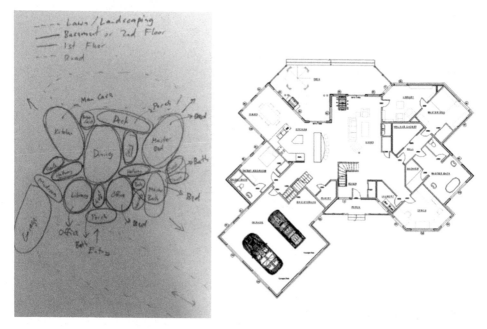

Image: Courtesy of Ryan Walker

Let's try an exercise. Below is a arial view of beautiful beach, imagine you are going to build a dream vacation home. Sketch out a bubble diagram of the spaces. What rooms need to be near each other, facing the ocean, etc.....?

Image: Google Earth

Sketch in the space above.

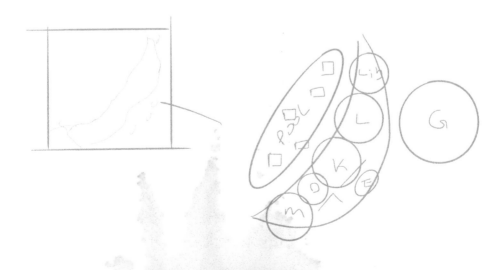

Always re-sketch the context. It gives you time to think and process your next move. The shape of the sand beach informs the banana-like shape of the house. Who said that houses need to be boxes? The Kitchen (K) centers the home with the Living Room (L) and the Library (Lib) on the right, with the Dining Room (D) and Master Bedroom (M) flanking the left. The Entrance (E) and Garage (G) are nestled on the forest side, with the main attraction—the pool on the ocean side—fronting the entire home. Inside the pool are square platforms contrasting the organic shape of the building and its context, while also mimicking the idea of islands floating in the ocean.

THE CONCEPT SKETCH

The final sketching technique is the concept sketch. It draws on all the lessons learned in the previous chapter and combines them with the thumbnail sketch, only on a larger scale (about the size of the palm of your hand). The goal of the concept sketch is to hone in on your idea. It is not about the numbers of drawings or iterations, like the thumbnail sketch. It is about conveying an idea in a more convincing manner.

For example, Genevieve DeGrandchamp was a freshman in our engineering drafting course. For her final project, she chose to design a staircase that needed replacement at the University of Colorado. Many students at the school are very outdoor oriented. Her inspiration was climbing gear used commonly at the nearby Flatiron Mountains. Her concept sketch brings you into her world.

The final result was produced in the Autodesk program Revit, and her images can be seen on the following pages.

Do you have a project you are working on, an idea mulling in the recesses of your mind that needs resurrecting? Try drawing a concept

sketch.

Sketch in the space below. Boil a project down to its essence and express that in your sketch.

I keep pushing you to draw because it is the best way to learn. You will pick up more by putting pen to paper than you will from me telling or showing you. The lesson will sink in and become rooted in your experiences, thus becoming more powerful for you.

Bring your thoughts and ideas out onto the paper. That way you can start to evaluate them. Create processes, assess with principles, explore and start designing your life. It is not about the result but the shape of the process. Designing a great process and you will have created an amazing life!

Find more training at:
Alexanderkgore.com/bookresources

References

REFERENCES

1   http://www.merriam-webster.com/dictionary/creativity

2   Tina Seelig: The 6 Characteristics of Truly Creative People. (n.d.).
    Retrieved May 02, 2016, from http://ed.ted.com/on/M4ZoDQqr

3   Green, R. (n.d.). Watch "The key to transforming yourself -- Robert
    Greene at TEDxBrixton" Video at TEDxTalks. Retrieved May
    02, 2016, from http://tedxtalks.ted.com/video/The-key-to-
    transforming-yoursel

4   Straker, D. (n.d.). Divergence and Convergence. Retrieved May 03,
    2016, from http://creatingminds.org/principles/div_conv.htm

5   Straker, D. (n.d.). Exploration. Retrieved May 03, 2016, from http://
    creatingminds.org/principles/exploration.html

6   McKee, R. (1997). Story: Substance, structure, style and the
    principles of screenwriting. New York: ReganBooks.

7   Roth, K. (2000, August 21). Fractals for the complete idiot. Retrieved
    May 07, 2016, from http://www.tonkoppens.nl/Tutorial01/test.html

8   Fibonacci Fractals. (n.d.). Retrieved May 07, 2016, from http://
    fractalfoundation.org/OFC/OFC-11-2.html

9   M. S., N. M., E. L., & P. L. (n.d.). New Frontiers in the Design of
    Integrated Exterior Wall Systems (Tech.). CTBUH.

10 Ferris, T. (2016,01). Tim Ferris Podcast: Chris Sacca on Shark Tank,
    Building Your Business, and Startup Mistakes [Audio podcast].
    Retrieved from http://itunes.apple.com

11 James, M. (n.d.). Refining Straw Bale R-values. Retrieved May 16,
    2016, from http://www.homeenergy.org/show/article/nav/
    walls/page/4/id/1456

12 Aurelius, Marcus. Meditations. London: Penguin, 2004. Print. Pg. 59

13 McKee, Robert. Story: Substance, Structure, Style and the Principles of Screenwriting. London: Methuen, 1997. Print.

14 "1997-98 NBA Leaders | Basketball-Reference.com." Basketball-Reference.com. Web. 27 May 2016.

15 "1997–98 Utah Jazz Season." - Wikipedia, the Free Encyclopedia. Web. 27 May 2016.

16 Manfred, Tony. "LeBron James Wants To Get Rid Of NBA Salary Limits, And Michael Jordan's Insane 1998 Salary Is The Reason Why." Business Insider. Business Insider, Inc, 2014. Web. 27 May 2016.

17 "What Is a Strategy? Definition and Meaning." BusinessDictionary. com. Web. 27 May 2016.

18 Http://www.youtube.com/channel/UCJ-CzMn3WFlZmnv0GAyK5uA. "Will Smith Motivational Speech- The Key To Life - Running and Reading." YouTube. YouTube, 2013. Web. 27 May 2016.

19 "Jamie Foxx on Workout Routines, Success Habits, and Untold Hollywood Stories." The Blog of Author Tim Ferriss. Web. 27 May 2016.

20 McCue, TJ. "Why Infographics Rule." Forbes. Forbes Magazine, 8 Jan. 2013. Web. 27 May 2016.

FOR MORE INFORMATION ABOUT THE AUTHOR:

BOOK: www.alexandergore.com
ARCHITECTURE: www.f9productions.com
TINY HOUSE: www.atlastinyhouse.com
REVIT: www.revitfurniture.com

Nature builds complexity from simplicity. You can too.

- Alex Gore

CPSIA information can be obtained
at www.ICGtesting.com
Printed in the USA
FSOW04n0730140916
24924FS